BRAIN HEALTH PUZZLES FOR ADULTS 2

CROSSWORDS, SUDOKU, AND OTHER PUZZLES THAT GIVE THE BRAIN THE EXERCISE IT NEEDS

PHIL FRAAS

Andrews McMeel
PUBLISHING®

Also by Phil Fraas

Brain Health Puzzles for Adults: Crosswords, Sudoku, and Other Puzzles That Give the Brain the Exercise It Needs

Andrews McMeel Publishing
a division of Andrews McMeel Universal
1130 Walnut Street, Kansas City, Missouri 64106

www.andrewsmcmeel.com

23 24 25 26 27 MCN 10 9 8 7 6 5 4 3 2 1

ISBN: 978-1-5248-8051-4

Editor: Patty Rice
Art Director: Julie Barnes
Production Editor: Elizabeth A. Garcia
Production Manager: Julie Skalla

ATTENTION: SCHOOLS AND BUSINESSES
Andrews McMeel books are available at quantity discounts with bulk purchase for educational, business, or sales promotional use. For information, please e-mail the Andrews McMeel Publishing Special Sales Department: sales@amuniversal.com.

INTRODUCTION

Staying active is about more than just your body; the brain needs regular exercise too . The consistent refrain from doctors and scientists studying brain health is, "Use it or lose it." And study after study shows that adults who exercise their brains fare better on tests measuring cognition, memory, and other indicia of brain health.

Where and how do we get that brain exercise we need? We can look to such activities as learning new things, keeping the mind active through social interaction, and working on puzzles and games to enhance cognitive fitness as important parts of our exercise regimen.

Further, it is good to challenge yourself as you exercise your brain. Don't limit yourself to exercise that you already are comfortable with; it helps to try things that really challenge your skills. You also benefit from putting some variety into your exercises. You won't get bored doing the same thing over and over again and you will be exercising different sets of mental "muscles." Experts believe that you maximize your brain exercise benefits by using as many different cognitive functions as possible.

This book, like the original *Brain Health Puzzles for Adults: Crosswords, Sudoku, and Other Puzzles That Give the Brain the Exercise It Needs,* is designed to aid you in your brain exercises. Its puzzles enable you to challenge yourself and use different mental facilities as you exercise.

This new volume follows the same organization as the original, and the two books look very similar. But this book is not a clone of the first. Far from it; all the puzzles and trivia questions in this book are freshly minted, not repeats.

The puzzles come in seven different flavors, divided between four types of word puzzles and three types of number logic puzzles, chosen to ensure that you are able to exercise a wide variety of your mental "muscles" as you work through them. The puzzles include crosswords, Sudoku, word searches, narrative logic puzzles, cryptograms, and two fun types of number logic puzzles—Calcudoku and Futoshiki—that are somewhat akin to Sudoku. If you are not familiar with any of these puzzle types, that's okay. It means you will have the chance to learn something new, which in itself is good brain exercise.

Chapter 1 introduces each type of puzzle with a sample puzzle, along with a discussion of brain health benefits involved in working on it, the basics of how to work that type of puzzle, and some solving hacks you might use as you work on developing your expertise in solving that type of puzzle. The material refines and augments the Chapter 1 presentation of the original *Brain Health Puzzles for Adults.*

Chapters 2, 3, and 4 all include suites of puzzles of each of the seven types. As you progress through the book, you will graduate from puzzles on the easier side (Chapter 2) to medium (Chapter 3) to more challenging (Chapter 4). This gradation of difficulty gives you the chance to develop your puzzling skills before you tackle the tougher puzzles that stretch your mental "muscles" the most. And it enables you to push your limits as the difficulty level increases, which serves to strengthen your brain's cognitive functions. Just in case, the solutions to all the puzzles (along with answers to several trivia questions that pop up throughout the book) are provided in a final chapter (see page 137).

In constructing the puzzles for this book, I strived to make sure that solvers will find them fun to work—accessible to those who aren't already expert puzzlers, and with engaging themes and clues for all who work on them. Who says you can't have fun while engaging in the brain exercise you need? So, get comfortable, sharpen your pencil, and get ready to enjoy a plentitude of word and number puzzles that are as fun as they are challenging.

CHAPTER 1
GETTING STARTED

CROSSWORDS

BRAIN HEALTH EXERCISE: long-term memory, attention to detail, logic

Figuring out what word fits into a crossword based on the fragmentary information available (including the number of letters in the entry, possibly one or more letters already in place, and the description of the entry in the clues) can really give your brain a workout. You will need to apply logic to determine what your options are, given the parameters you are working with. Then, you will have to rely heavily on your long-term memory to recall the word or phrase that best fits that entry. Also, you will find that many clues are not synonyms for, or bland definitions of, the entry but are indirect descriptions that require the application of logic to figure out what word the puzzle constructor is pointing you toward.

HOW TO SOLVE: It is straightforward—you must fill in all the blank squares on the puzzle grid by completing every Across and Down entry, using the information provided in the set of clues that accompanies the grid.

TIPS FOR SOLVING

» Establish footholds right away. At the beginning, scan the entire list of clues looking for "low-hanging fruit," that is, entries you can fill in right away. Then, if you can, use those entries to create footholds—a small grouping of entries built around the first one. Eventually, you will create and expand enough footholds that they cross-fertilize one another and even the most difficult and longest entries will become solvable.

» Don't get bogged down. Once you have done all you can to build on a foothold but can't do anymore, go work on creating another foothold somewhere else on the grid and come back to this area later. I do that a lot. It keeps my frustration at a minimum and my attitude positive; I prefer spending my time looking for opportunities rather than spinning my wheels at a temporary roadblock.

» Take the hints. For the many clues that are not simply synonyms for or definitions of the entry, be on the lookout for what the puzzle constructor is asking. For example, in a medium or more challenging puzzle for which the constructor doesn't include in the clue information that the entry is an abbreviation of a word, or an acronym, or other set of initials, the clue will hint at that by including an abbreviation in the clue. "Lawyers' org." as the clue to fit a three-square slot is not asking you to try to enter "American Bar Association" but wants you to write in "ABA." Another sort of hint embedded in the clue "Night, in Nogales" is really asking for the Spanish word for "night," that is, NOCHE.

» Look out for the occasional clue ending in a question mark. It doesn't mean that the constructor is unsure whether the clue is a valid one or not; rather it means that the clue might involve some outrageous pun usually associated with the puzzle's theme or that it is very misdirecting. As an example of the latter, if the clue is "Repeat performance?", the answer might be ECHO because the essence of an echo is that it repeats a sound being uttered. Convoluted, yes; unfair, no; fun when you figure it out, yes.

» What happens when you encounter an entry for which the answer is just not stored in your brain's memory bank? I've kept the number of truly obscure words to just a tiny handful. But, in case you run into an entry that is a real stumper, you can get the answer you are looking for by filling in all the crossing entries, which I try to make sure aren't so obscure. Plus, at the end of the process, you will have learned a new word!

ACROSS

1. Aromas
6. Golf standards
10. Broke bread
13. Poe bird
14. Black ink item
15. Third degree?
16. A nickname for Ireland
18. Hawaiian floral necklace
19. Colorful wraps
20. Dulles, for one
22. Close-fitting
23. California's ____ Sur
24. BBs, e.g.
25. Brewpub offering
27. Hawaiian naval base
30. Chicken ____
32. Genetic initials
33. Not just "a"
34. Spring month
36. "____ Maria"
38. South American range
42. Opposite of paleo-
44. Letter accompanier: Abbr.
46. Hawaiian tuber
47. Restaurant chain named for a Rolling Stones hit
52. Still
53. Carbon compound
54. Blasting stuff: Init.
55. 007
57. Epicure's condiment
59. Athena's Roman counterpart
62. Tabby
63. Hawaiian landmark near Waikiki
65. Bring into play
66. Herb with a licorice-like flavor
67. Obliterate
68. Always, to the poet
69. Liquefy
70. Cow's first stomach

DOWN

1. Valuable rocks
2. Lady's title
3. Boss
4. Put on TV again
5. Quickly and eagerly buy
6. Chi follower
7. Tear into
8. Ignite again
9. Suffix with gang or mob
10. Poise
11. Heat: Comb. form
12. Newspaper VIP
14. Commercials
17. French cubist
21. Mom or dad
23. Most valiant
25. Letters preceding an alias
26. Back talk
28. Santa ____, California
29. Triumphant cry
31. Certain plastics
35. Permit
37. Football lineman
39. Reverie
40. Bard's "before"
41. Toper
43. Silhouette, essentially
45. Log home
47. Save from peril
48. Disquiet
49. Straw hat
50. Involve
51. Wild blue _____
56. India's first PM
58. Genesis name
59. Homer's bartender
60. Arrangement holder
61. Yemeni city
64. Colorado clock setting: Init.

№1 REAL GEMS

1	2	3	4	5	■	6	7	8	9	■	10	11	12
13				■	14				■	15		
16				17				■	18			
19				■	20			21				
■	22			■	23		■	24				
25	26		■	27		28			29			
30			31	■	32			33			■	■
34			35	■	36		37	■	38		39	40	41
■	42		43	■	44		45	■	46			
47	48	49		■	50			51	■	52		
53			■	54			55		56		■	■
57			58		■	59				60	61	
62		■	63		64				■			
65		■	66				■	67				
68		■	69			■		70				

THINK ABOUT IT

The achievement of solving a puzzle, or even just a difficult part of a puzzle, produces dopamine in the body. Dopamine is a neurotransmitter that regulates mood, memory, and concentration; generally it provides a positive boost to your mood and makes you feel relaxed and at ease. No wonder people like to work on puzzles.

BRAIN HEALTH EXERCISE: attention to detail, spatial abilities, short-term working memory

While not complicated to work on, word searches can give you a great deal of brain exercise. To successfully complete one, you need to rely heavily on your short-term working memory as you visually toggle between the list of key words and the puzzle grid and then scan the grid looking for the key word or words you have in mind. Since the puzzle's key words can be embedded in the grid any which way, you also will have to draw on your brain's spatial functions to spot those harder-to-envision words. Finally, great attention to detail is required; it is easy to pass over what you are looking for when scanning the grid unless you keep focused.

HOW TO SOLVE: Scan the puzzle grid to find all the words in the key words list below the grid. Mark each word both on the grid and in the key words list as you find it by circling or striking through it.

TIPS FOR SOLVING

» First and foremost, keep in mind that the word you are looking for in the grid can be embedded in any of eight different ways: forward, backward, vertically, upside-down, slanted diagonally from left to right or right to left, and reading from the top to the bottom or vice versa.

» Visual scanning techniques: I believe that a lot of it is personal preference. All I can do is tell you what I prefer, but with the caveat that might not be the way your brain works for scanning things. I prefer to go across each row or down each column looking for a key letter. Typically, the first letter in the word. No preference as to how many rows or columns to scan at the same time. Sometimes, I feel like I want to take on just one at a time; on other occasions, when I am feeling really sharp, I might try as many as three adjoining rows/columns at a time.

» Alternatively (and I do it this way sometimes as a change of pace), you can scan the grid more generally looking for letters that pop right out to you. For me those are Os and Qs. For you, it might be Is or Ts.

» An efficient way to scan the grid, though it is very demanding of your short-term working memory, is to pick several words with the same first letter and scan the grid for all of them at the same time.

» Usually, one starts the scanning process by looking for words by first letter, but if that doesn't fully pan out, you might try looking for some other letter in the key word, one that might be easy to scan for, like an O. And if you feel ambitious, you can try to scan for other key words you are having trouble locating that contain this letter.

№1 ITALY

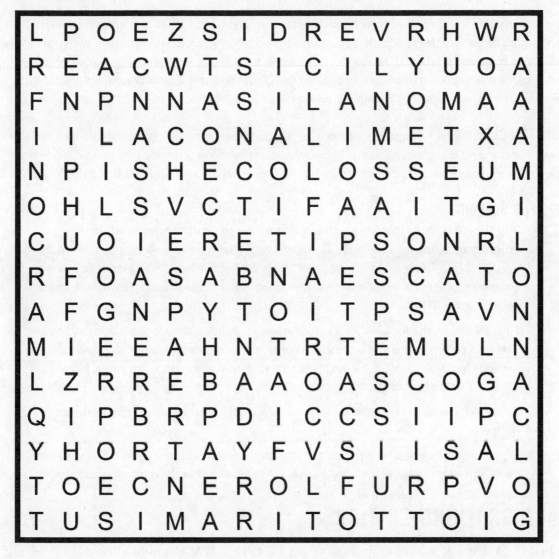

```
L P O E Z S I D R E V R H W R
R E A C W T S I C I L Y U O A
F N P N N A S I L A N O M A A
I I L A C O N A L I M E T X A
N P I S H E C O L O S S E U M
O H L S V C T I F A A I T G I
C U O I E R E T I P S O N R L
R F O A S A B N A E S C A T O
A F G N P Y T O I T P S A V N
M I E E A H N T R T E M U L N
L Z R R E B A A O A S C O G A
Q I P B R P D I C C S I I P C
Y H O R T A Y F V S I I S A L
T O E C N E R O L F U R P V O
T U S I M A R I T O T T O I G
```

AUTOSTRADA	FLORENCE	PASTA	SISTINE CHAPEL
CAESAR	GIOTTO	PISA	THE BOOT
CANNOLI	LA SCALA	POMPEII	TIRAMISU
CHIANTI	MARCONI	"PREGO"	TUSCANY
"CIAO"	MILAN	RENAISSANCE	UFFIZI gallery
COLOSSEUM	MONA LISA	RICOTTA	VENICE
FERRARI	MT. ETNA	ROME	VERDI
FIAT	PANCETTA	SICILY	VESPA

BRAIN HEALTH EXERCISE: logic, long-term memory, pattern recognition

The code used in a cryptogram (which is a straightforward substitution of one letter for another) can only be broken by the application of creative thinking/inductive logic, combined with use of your long-term memory of how English words and sentences are structured. Decoding also involves the use of pattern recognition (looking for repeated use of certain letter combinations), as you develop hypotheses as to what various encoded groups of letters might mean.

HOW TO SOLVE: Each cryptogram consists of an encoded quotation of something said by a well-known person and that person's name. To help you get started, we offer you hints that decode from one to three letters used in the cryptogram, but you don't have to use the hints if you don't want to.

TIPS FOR SOLVING

» You should start by looking for clues given by the structure of the words in the cryptogram. Look for one-letter words or words that have an apostrophe toward the end. That one-letter word is an A or I 99.9 percent of the time, and a letter following an apostrophe most likely is an S or T. In a two-letter word that starts with a T, the second letter likely is an O.

» I am always on the lookout for a three-letter word that is positioned like it might be THE and testing out those letters in other parts of the cryptogram. Also, be on the lookout for letter combinations that might suggest a common noun suffix, like -TION or -ENCE in longer words.

» Be sure to check to see whether a word is repeated in the puzzle, as that commonly happens.

» Don't forget the title of the puzzle. It might give you a good hint as you try to visualize, even with a lot of gaps in the wording, what the overall text of the quotation is driving at.

№1 A SCATHING CRITIQUE

BJLH ORVLKFHNCZ NK EJZP UJJI RVI JHNUNVRG; ELZ

_____

ZPM CRHZ ZPRZ NK UJJI NK VJZ JHNUNVRG, RVI ZPM

_____

CRHZ ZPRZ NK JHNUNVRG NK VJZ UJJI.

_____

—KROLMG XJPVKJV

_____

HINTS (SEE PAGE 138): 26, 36, 38

SUDOKU

BRAIN HEALTH EXERCISE: logic, attention to detail, short-term working memory

Solving a Sudoku primarily is an exercise in deductive logic, determining with certainty, in each case, that a cell in the grid can contain one and only one out of the nine possible digits. It also involves great attention to detail and use of your short-term working memory as you try to confirm a number's place in a cell, which might involve two or more steps in the analytical process. Then, when all the easy wins are gotten, one must get creative and use inductive logic to spot potential pathways to determining a number's spot on the grid.

HOW TO SOLVE: To solve a Sudoku, you must fill each empty cell in the grid with a number 1 through 9, so that each row across, each column down, and each 3x3 "cage" contains all the numbers 1 through 9 with no repeats.

TIPS FOR SOLVING

» It usually is good to start by working through each numeral from 1 through 9 to see whether the grid already contains enough iterations of that numeral that one can deduce where one or more of the other iterations of that numeral must appear.

» Then, I prefer to use the "rule of five," under which I look for a row, column, or cage already filled with five or more of the numbers 1 through 9 and then see whether I can deduce where one or more of the remaining four or fewer numbers must go based on the layout of filled cells at that time. This process stands a reasonable chance of yielding a determination as to the location of at least one, but possibly more, of the remaining numbers. This technique won't work for a few more difficult Sudoku in which you don't have any clusters of five to work with; however, for most puzzles, I think this process gets you to a solved puzzle more quickly.

» Once the first two processes are completed, then it is a matter of analyzing the information now on the grid (including the info you have added) to look for further solutions, based on pure logic.

SUDOKU №1

	4		5					
	7	9			2			
5		3			9			7
		2	8	9		7		3
				3				
3		6		5	7	1		
4			9			8		2
			1			9	7	
				4		5		

BRAIN HEALTH EXERCISE: logic, short-term working memory

Solving a Calcudoku requires the use of deductive logic to determine with certainty in what order the numbers in a row or column must appear, using the grid "cages" and inserts as a starting point. In some instances, you also likely will have to use inductive logic to develop hypotheses as to what numbers could fit into a cage. Relying on your short-term working memory, you try out your hypotheses in your head. If one doesn't work, you go on to try other combinations until you find the right one.

HOW TO SOLVE: Calcudoku is a number logic puzzle like Sudoku but differs in that its puzzle grid doesn't have any seeded numbers already inserted in the grid. Rather, the grid is filled with "cages" that vary in size, and each cage has inserted in the upper-left corner a number with an arithmetic symbol indicating addition, subtraction, multiplication, or division (the symbol for which in this book is :, not ÷). That insert tells you that when you apply the arithmetic function to the numbers you propose to insert in the cage, they must result in the insert number. Single-cell cages simply designate the number that is intended to go in the cell.

TIPS FOR SOLVING

» Start by filling in the "slam dunk" single-cell cages right away and then pencil in lightly (because you don't know what order they will appear in the grid) numbers in cages that can contain only those numbers. For example, a two-cell cage with an insert reading "15x" can only contain 3 and 5 in one or the other order.

» Next, look for any information you have in a crossing row or column that can confirm where, in the 15x example, the 3 and 5 belong within the 15x cage.

» Then, it is a matter of winkling out every number placement that the limited information in the grid will support and you can spot.

» Don't forget that you can always put your review of the cages aside and apply the most basic Sudoku technique of scanning each row and column of the grid that has some filled-in numbers to see whether an obvious placement of another number in an empty cell of that row or column is in order.

CALCUDOKU №1

12×		2×	
2 :		9+	4+
3 :			
	1-		4

FUTOSHIKI

BRAIN HEALTH EXERCISE: logic, spatial abilities, short-term working memory

Solving a Futoshiki requires application of deductive logic, along with spatial reasoning, as you visually follow inequality signs that connect cells in different columns and rows of the grid. As the puzzles increase in difficulty, they also require you to use inductive logic and to lean heavily on your short-term working memory as you try to picture in your mind what the consequences might be of opting for a choice in number placement.

HOW TO SOLVE: A Futoshiki, like Sudoku and Calcudoku, is a number logic puzzle. What distinguishes it is that it differs in that its puzzle grid doesn't have a bunch of seeded numbers already inserted in the grid (as with Sudoku), nor does it use "cages" within the grid (as with Calcudoku) to convey information about missing numbers—instead, it uses a few seeded numbers and strategically placed inequality signs (>) to show what order the numbers should appear in the completed grid. For example, 3 followed by a > to the right of it on the grid means that the number to the right of it can only be a 2 or a 1.

TIPS FOR SOLVING

» A 1 can never be larger than another number and, if the grid measures 6x6, a 6 can never be smaller than another number. So, a good way to start is to scan the rows and columns looking for these minimum or maximum situations that indirectly tell you where a 1 or 6 must go.

» Focus on extended series of connected inequality signs. If you can peg the number in a cell in that sequence, you gain a lot of information on what the other numbers in the sequence might be.

» As with Calcudoku, don't forget that you can put your review of the inequality signs aside and apply the most basic Sudoku technique of scanning each row and column of the grid with some filled-in numbers to see whether an obvious placement of another number in an empty cell of that row or column is in order.

FUTOSHIKI №1

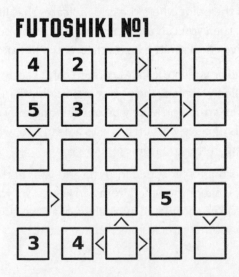

BRAIN HEALTH EXERCISE: deductive logic, spatial reasoning, attention to detail

Narrative logic puzzles involve the application of deductive logic to facts reflected in or implied by the puzzle's clues, i.e., if a car color can't be green, blue, or red, it must be the only option left—white. Also, while the logic puzzle grid is a powerful tool to enable you to solve the puzzle, to take advantage of it, you must be able to deduce what the data points on it created by the negative check marks and positive stars tell you about other empty boxes in it, which really puts a premium on spatial reasoning. Scrupulous attention to detail, however, is equally critical to successfully filling out a Logic Puzzle grid and, thus, solving the puzzle. Many times, I have found that I missed one small detail in a clue that, once it is brought into play, creates a domino effect leading to my gaining further information on a number of related details, or I made a mistake in marking up the grid that makes the grid worthless.

HOW TO SOLVE: Narrative logic puzzles ask you to tie together various items in several categories based on fragmentary statements about the items provided as clues. Essential to working a logic puzzle is the grid, which converts the narrative information stated in, or deduced from, the clues into abstract spatial concepts. The grid is constructed so that each item in each category is matched with every other item in every other category once (but only once) in a box on the grid. You use it by putting checks or Xs in boxes that you know are false ("Jim's car is not blue.") and stars in the boxes you determine to be true ("Joe's car is or must be a Ford."). The conversion process of posting negative checkmarks and positive stars on the grid enables you to use the information you have extracted from the clues to deduce, based solely on the positioning of the filled-in boxes in the grid, conclusions about options the clues don't themselves address. That, in turn, allows you to fill in further boxes, and eventually you end up with every box on the grid filled with a negative checkmark or positive star. Then, you convert all positive stars on the grid back into the nonabstract connections, which form the answer to the puzzle.

TIPS FOR SOLVING

» As the grid fills with negative check marks and some positive stars, use your spatial reasoning to reach deductive conclusions that allow you to place a positive star next to an item without there having been a positive statement about the item—or perhaps even any statement directly touching on the item—in the list of clues. For example, if you get to the point where the grid indicates that Jim's car is red and that the red car is a Chevy, then you can put a positive star in the box that matches Jim and Chevy and negative checks in the boxes that match Jim and other car brands.

» Focus, focus, focus! Did you read the clues correctly and capture all the ramifications of a clue on the grid? Did you place the negative check mark in the correct box in the grid? If you mess up, the error won't likely be obvious and only after working a lot further in your analysis of clues will you come to a dead end, which means you will have to start over filling in the grid from scratch.

» Keep in mind that information encoded into the grid later in the analysis can reshape the significance of information provided from early clues; so, you should go back over the clues again once you've completed an analysis of all the clues and marked up the grid initially to see what other conclusions you can reach.

№1 APPLE-PICKING CONTEST

It is the early fall apple harvesting season, and a local farmer who has many acres of apple trees bursting with fruit is donating some of his production to charity. Before he sends his workers to harvest the crop, he has allowed the nearby food bank to send four energetic young volunteers out to the farm to spend a morning picking as many apples as they can in three hours, with the apples they pick going to the food bank free of charge. The four volunteers have decided to make a contest out of it, seeing which one can pick the most weight in apples during the allotted time. The farm has four apple orchards, and one volunteer went to each orchard to do their picking. The clues below provide some information on how the contest went and who won it. See whether you can read the clues to extract that info.

1. The contestants included Adam, the guy who worked the River Bend orchard, the one who picked 1,130 pounds of apples in the three allotted hours, and Art.

2. Allan didn't pick the most or second-most poundage of apples.

3. Art didn't do his apple picking at either the Farm Road orchard or the South 40 orchard, nor did he pull down 1,010 pounds of apples.

4. Adrian was not assigned to the South 40 orchard; and the volunteer who picked 930 pounds of apples in the contest didn't do so at the River Bend orchard.

		Orchard				Pounds Picked			
		Farm Road	Old Barn	River Bend	South 40	850	930	1,010	1,130
Picker	Adam								
	Adrian								
	Allan								
	Art								
Pounds Picked	850								
	930								
	1,010								
	1,130								

CHAPTER 2
PUZZLES ON THE EASIER SIDE

CROSSWORD

ACROSS

1. Show flexibility
6. Unwanted e-mail
10. Greek cheese
14. Actress Winger
15. Jason's ship
16. Figure skater's jump
17. Anagram for COORDINATE
19. Cylindrical farm storage structure
20. Discussion venue
21. Spill the beans
23. Private, when encountering an officer
26. Stow, as cargo
27. Currier's partner in lithography
28. Anagram for STAGNATION
33. Skin problem
35. Consumer
36. ____-Locka, Fla.
37. Bummed
38. Like Hammett's falcon
41. GOPer's opponent, briefly
42. Versatile truck, informally
43. Miners' finds
44. Glisten
46. Anagram for SUPERSONIC
50. Means justifiers, it is said
51. General ____ chicken
52. Most high-minded
54. (Has) emerged
57. Drive away
58. Assorted: Abbr.
59. Anagram for INDISCREET
64. First name in scat
65. Spill the beans
66. Claw
67. (Has) espied
68. Puff of a joint
69. Tour of duty

DOWN

1. Do sums
2. Ruby or Sandra
3. Epitome of simplicity
4. Copious
5. Divination deck of cards
6. Second-largest planet
7. Straitlaced and demure
8. In the past
9. Pictorial composites
10. Attach firmly
11. Off-ramp
12. Spill the beans
13. Skin soother
18. Field
22. Is wild about
23. Shows sudden interest, metaphorically
24. Fly a plane
25. Role that a bank often plays
26. Cut with a light beam
29. Rwandan people
30. First-aid item
31. Shells out
32. Most subdued
34. "Are you a man or _____?"
39. Fire-starting felon
40. More or ____
45. WWII carrier-based fighter plane
47. Type of medical X-ray
48. Jittery
49. "Forget it!"
53. Outdoes
54. Home of Iowa State
55. Stir to anger
56. ____ of Capri
57. Skaters' venue
60. Carnaval site
61. Biblical high priest
62. Oui's opposite
63. Big bang maker: Init.

№2 ANAGRAMS

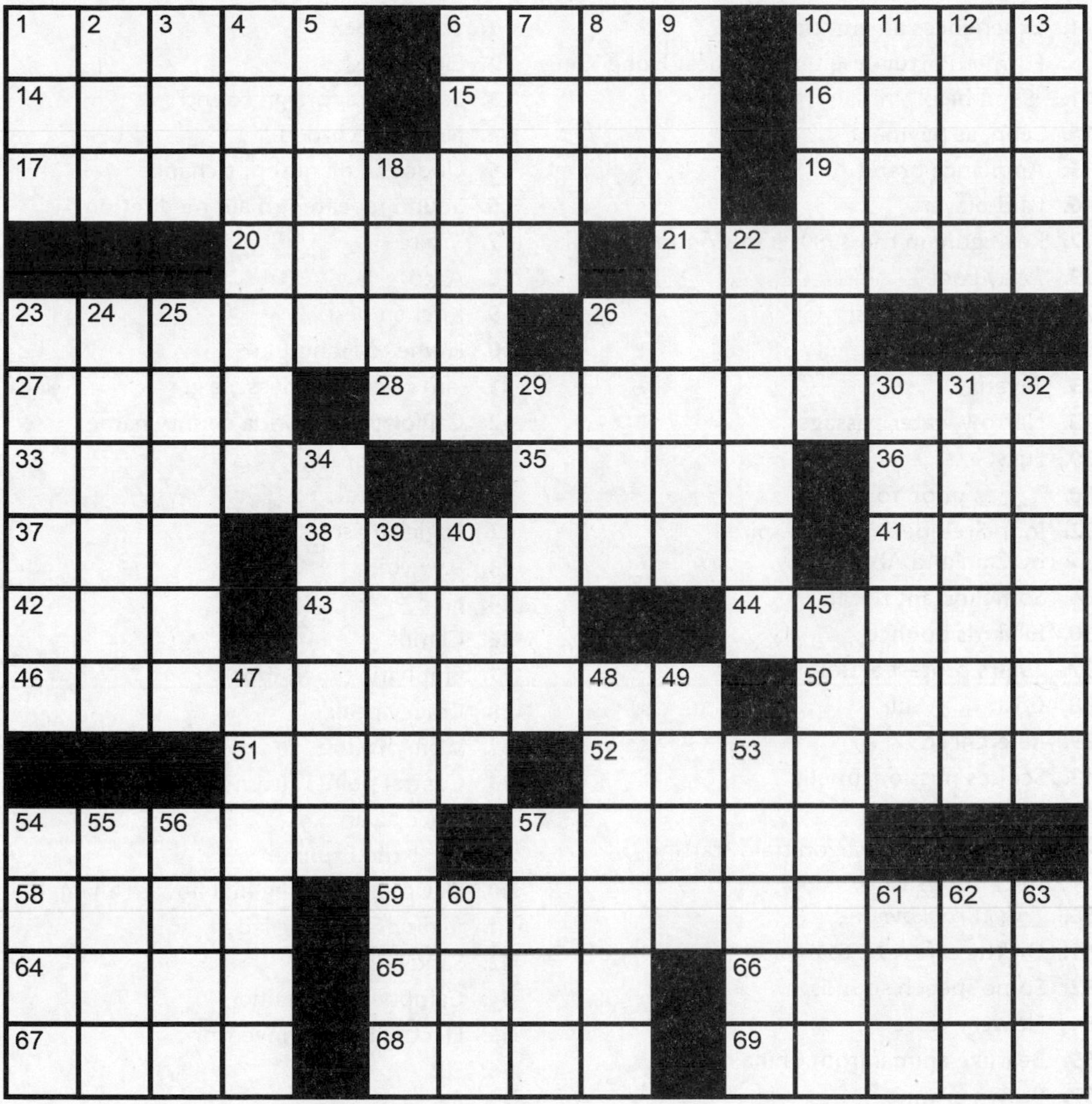

DID YOU KNOW?

An interesting finding scientists have made about memory is referred to as the "reminiscence bump." Adults over 40 tend to remember more about events that occurred when they were between the ages of 15 and 25 than any other period of their lives; and when the data showing that is plotted on a graph, it looks like a big bump in the timeline. Not surprising though, given that those years are a pretty intense part of everyone's life.

ACROSS

1. Experiences an emotion
6. Former Portuguese territory near Hong Kong
11. "Send help!" initials
14. Send, as payment
15. Appliance brand
16. Paid player
17. Key figure in the 1980s Iran-Contra scandal
19. "Way cool!"
20. Insinuate, suggest
21. Flip over
23. Tavern
25. Narrow water passage
29. Fury
30. "____, poor Yorick!"
32. John Steinbeck novel inspired by Cain and Abel's story
34. Some instant decafs
36. Billiards bounce
37. 1960's protest action
38. Costa ____ Sol
39. Referenced
43. Scout's mission, briefly
45. Hindu deity
46. Cry heard on a wagon train starting the journey to Oregon
50. ____ Brockovich
51. On the safe side, to a tar
52. Some speech sounds
54. Flowery verse
55. Bearlike animal from China
57. Brown ermine
59. "___ show time!"
60. Long Island town that is a vacation enclave for the rich and famous
66. Golf bag item
67. Dated
68. Donnybrook
69. Driver's lic. and others: Init.
70. Anagram for PESTS
71. Apply, as pressure

DOWN

1. To's partner
2. Electric fish
3. Settler in a foreign country
4. Not prerecorded
5. Undoes a manuscript change
6. Sound repeated to aid meditation
7. "Yo te ___"
8. Auto
9. Kitchen pest
10. Home to Honolulu
11. Jam or cream cheese, e.g.
12. California or Florida county name
13. Soaked through
18. Assigns stars to
22. Logician's start
23. Low voice
24. Jai ____
26. Climbs
27. Emphatic type: Abbr.
28. Craggy peak
31. Went around
33. Central points (from the Latin)
35. Once again
38. ____ the Explorer
40. Device controlling fuel flow to an engine
41. Idylls of the King lady
42. Sandy ridge
44. Campbell's container
45. Electric battery inventor
46. Elk
47. Jubilant
48. Has a hunch
49. ###
53. WWI battle site
56. Egyptian snakes
58. Peak
61. Feedbag morsel
62. Employ
63. Cooking measure: Abbr.
64. Across, to a bard
65. After expenses

№3 DIRECTIONS

1	2	3	4	5	■	6	7	8	9	10	■	11	12	13
14					■	15					■	16		
17					18						■	19		
■	■	20					■	■	21	22				
23	24		■	25			26	27	28	■	29			
30			31		32				33					
34				35		■	36				■	■	■	■
37				■	38			■	39		40	41	42	
■	■	43		44				45						
46	47	48					49		■	50				
51				■	52			53	■	54				
55			56	■	■	57			58	■	■			
59			■	60	61	62	63					64	65	
66			67				■	68						
69			70				■	71						

THINK ABOUT IT

"Don't stay sheltered in your comfort zone." That's the advice some scientists give those working puzzles or making other efforts to exercise their brains. The scientists stress the importance of taking on new challenges or increasing the difficulty level of things you already are familiar with as ways to get the most out of your brain exercise.

ACROSS

1. Happen
6. John, Paul, and John Paul
11. Big coffee holder
14. Public square
15. Oneness
16. New and different: Prefix
17. Radar, Anna, and race car, for three
19. Skillet
20. NBC sketch show, briefly
21. Expected
22. The Chrysler Building's style
24. Wears away
27. Whinnies
28. Plays a guitar
30. Japanese cartoon genre
32. Disney mermaid
33. Buttonhole, e.g.
34. Broadcast watchdog letters
37. Biopic of a rock and roll legend starring Gary Busey, with "The"
41. Loser to DDE twice
42. "I cannot tell _____"
43. Drakes, bucks, and boars
44. Binge
46. Missile
47. Far _____ (way off course)
50. Hightails it
52. Papyrus or cattail
54. Giant great
55. Contents of some barrels
58. Brest friend
59. Insultingly low compensation, in slang
62. Grassy area
63. Some metric weights, in short
64. Bar of precious metal
65. Hallucinogenic initials
66. Garden tool
67. Bridge positions

DOWN

1. Game adversaries, for short
2. Highlands family group
3. Phone screening aids
4. Israeli weapon
5. Haphazardly
6. Thick soup
7. Lennon's love
8. High-quality cotton
9. Forever and a day
10. The "S" in GPS
11. Remove, as a clothespin
12. Stretch (for)
13. They're verboten
18. Fizzlers
23. Run out of juice
25. Felt bad about
26. Sorties
28. Small Caribbean island known for its ecotourism
29. "How _____!"
31. Africa's longest river
33. One and only
34. Pete Seeger's forte
35. Canadian tribe
36. Dermatologist's concern
38. Privation
39. Blended fruit concoction
40. Diplomat's asset
44. Homily: Abbr.
45. Pulls off, as feathers from a chicken
46. Campus military org.: Init.
47. Have _____ (live it up)
48. Shows anger
49. Homeric epic
51. Small woods
53. Maui dance
56. "_____ Rhythm" (Gershwin tune)
57. "Shall we?" reply
60. Stylish, in the '60s
61. Carrier to Tokyo: Init.

№4 THE THREE AMIGOS

<table>
<tr><td>1</td><td>2</td><td>3</td><td>4</td><td>5</td><td>■</td><td>6</td><td>7</td><td>8</td><td>9</td><td>10</td><td>■</td><td>11</td><td>12</td><td>13</td></tr>
<tr><td>14</td><td></td><td></td><td></td><td></td><td>■</td><td>15</td><td></td><td></td><td></td><td></td><td>■</td><td>16</td><td></td><td></td></tr>
<tr><td>17</td><td></td><td></td><td></td><td>18</td><td></td><td></td><td></td><td></td><td></td><td></td><td>■</td><td>19</td><td></td><td></td></tr>
<tr><td>20</td><td></td><td></td><td>■</td><td>21</td><td></td><td></td><td>■</td><td>22</td><td></td><td></td><td>23</td><td></td><td></td><td></td></tr>
<tr><td>■</td><td>■</td><td>24</td><td>25</td><td></td><td></td><td>■</td><td>26</td><td></td><td>■</td><td>27</td><td></td><td></td><td></td><td></td></tr>
<tr><td>28</td><td>29</td><td></td><td></td><td></td><td></td><td>■</td><td>30</td><td>31</td><td></td><td></td><td>■</td><td>■</td><td>■</td><td>■</td></tr>
<tr><td>32</td><td></td><td></td><td></td><td>■</td><td>33</td><td></td><td></td><td></td><td>■</td><td>■</td><td>34</td><td>35</td><td>36</td><td></td></tr>
<tr><td>37</td><td></td><td></td><td>38</td><td></td><td></td><td></td><td></td><td>39</td><td>40</td><td></td><td></td><td></td><td></td><td></td></tr>
<tr><td>41</td><td></td><td>■</td><td>42</td><td></td><td></td><td></td><td>■</td><td>43</td><td></td><td></td><td></td><td></td><td></td><td></td></tr>
<tr><td>■</td><td>■</td><td>44</td><td>45</td><td></td><td></td><td>■</td><td>46</td><td></td><td></td><td></td><td></td><td>■</td><td>■</td><td>■</td></tr>
<tr><td>47</td><td>48</td><td>49</td><td></td><td></td><td>■</td><td>50</td><td>51</td><td></td><td></td><td></td><td>■</td><td>■</td><td>■</td><td>■</td></tr>
<tr><td>52</td><td></td><td></td><td></td><td>53</td><td>■</td><td>54</td><td></td><td></td><td>■</td><td>55</td><td>56</td><td>57</td><td></td><td></td></tr>
<tr><td>58</td><td></td><td>■</td><td>59</td><td></td><td>60</td><td></td><td></td><td></td><td>61</td><td></td><td></td><td></td><td></td><td></td></tr>
<tr><td>62</td><td></td><td>■</td><td>63</td><td></td><td></td><td>■</td><td>64</td><td></td><td></td><td></td><td></td><td></td><td></td><td></td></tr>
<tr><td>65</td><td></td><td>■</td><td>66</td><td></td><td></td><td>■</td><td>67</td><td></td><td></td><td></td><td></td><td></td><td></td><td></td></tr>
</table>

1950S TRIVIA CHALLENGE

What baseball team won more baseball World Series championships in the period 1950 – 1959 than any other team?

What was the most popular sitcom on TV in the 1950s?

ACROSS

1. Hook with a handle
5. Obligations
10. Rolling stone's lack
14. End in _____ (require overtime)
15. Wading bird
16. Spot of land in the ocean
17. California strait spanned by an iconic bridge
19. Ado
20. Did some CIA work
21. Avaricious
23. Natural wonder that lies at the foot of the Wasatch Mountains
26. Set up, schedule
28. Expanse
29. Country dance
30. Soon, to a bard
33. Competing
37. Honest ____
38. Weapon with a pin
40. *The Matrix* hero
41. Pesto base
43. Triumphant cry of accomplishment
44. Palindromic man's name
45. *Casablanca* pianist
47. Ailment
49. It has gouged some stunning western canyons
54. Doohickey placed on your finger as part of a medical checkup
55. Enter, as data
58. _____ Russo of *Get Shorty*
59. Mountainous area of California that includes scenic Mt. Whitney and Yosemite
62. Textile worker
63. Empathetic comment
64. _____ lily (Utah's state flower)
65. Sunday messages: Abbr.
66. Intuit
67. Canonized femmes: Abbr.

DOWN

1. Comedian's stock
2. At the peak of
3. Delicate ornamental works made with fine wire
4. Part of FBI
5. Lion's home
6. Breakfast staple
7. Boasts
8. Four: Prefix
9. Good buys, colloquially
10. Make a bad move
11. Port of ancient Rome
12. Move furtively
13. Twilled fabric
18. First family's home
22. Martin or Carell
24. Food thickener
25. Precept
26. Kuwaiti or Saudi
27. Musical McEntire
31. ____ roll (winning)
32. Low point
34. Explain the meaning of
35. Trawling equipment
36. Gunks
38. Menacing look
39. Limp watch painter
42. Chemically similar compounds
44. Unity
46. "Chances Are" crooner
48. 2023 Super Bowl's number
49. Woodpile units
50. Daisy variety
51. Sharply hit baseball
52. Prepare for a winter takeoff sometimes
53. Church keyboard instrument
56. Implore
57. New Mexico art community
60. Store posting: Abbr.
61. Perceive

№ 5 THE PICTURESQUE WEST

DID YOU KNOW?

It is estimated that there might be 500,000 or more words in the English language. But we don't carry that number of words around in our brains. It is said that the average personal vocabulary of an English-speaking adult is around 20,000 words. Many of the rest likely are scientific or technical terms not used very often.

ACROSS

1. Italian monk's title
4. Green gems
9. Cake topper
14. Corn unit
15. La Bohème, for one
16. Benefactor
17. 1920s saloon
19. Muscat native
20. Gawk
21. Bag-checking org.: Init.
23. Black, to the poet
24. Police evidence gatherers: Init.
27. Washington baseballers, briefly
29. Marco Polo crossed it
32. Unlimited authority, metaphorically
37. Touch down
38. Homer's sea
39. FDR-era agency: Init.
40. Medieval strings
42. Argentina neighbor: Abbr.
43. _____ Park, Colo.
45. Lyric poem
46. Often-unpaid worker
49. Short form for "Patricia" or "Leticia"
50. Nominal leader
52. Pro _____ (proportionally)
53. 66 and others: Abbr.
54. Tibetan priest
56. Hilo feast
58. Tennis match segment
61. One-time Fox News honcho Roger _____
65. Prefix for "mural" or "state"
67. Roast turkey part
70. Surgical tube
71. Buenos _____, Argentina
72. Diagnostic procedure: Init.
73. Sheriff's group
74. Word before Carlo or Cassino on maps
75. Word that can finish each part of 17-, 32-, 50-, and 67-Across

DOWN

1. Own (up to)
2. Enthralled
3. Side squared, for a square
4. One-liners, e.g.
5. Gorilla
6. Narc's org.: Init.
7. Prefix with "while"
8. Simon _____
9. Altar avowal
10. Biblical verb meaning "arrives"
11. One way to vote
12. Inadvisable action
13. Smile
18. Covered passageway
22. Singer/songwriter Paul _____
25. Basketball coaching great at Okla. State
26. Private detective, slangily
28. Teen affliction
29. _____ the above
30. Riyadh resident
31. Blends together
33. Concur
34. Relating to the nervous system
35. Colgate rival
36. Buckwheat cereal
41. Filly's father
44. Narrow waterway
47. Famed loch
48. Confidentiality contract, for short
51. 180's
55. Billiard shot
56. Talk like Daffy
57. Golden Rule preposition
59. Dutch cheese
60. Duet plus one
62. Fancy wheels
63. Anagram for CURE
64. Comedy sketch
66. Devoured
68. Decorative vase
69. Encountered

№6 FINISHING TOUCH

(crossword grid)

THINK ABOUT IT

Eating foods rich in antioxidants, such as blueberries and other dark berries, dark chocolate, and green teas, is said to be good for the brain. The antioxidants help the body ameliorate the damaging effects on tissues caused by free radicals (unstable atoms in the body), which otherwise can lead to functional decline in aging brains.

ACROSS

1. Trite
6. A Simpson
10. "Dancing Queen" group
14. Thumb _____ (hitchhike)
15. Plains native
16. Make ready, briefly
17. What an incomplete pass on first and ten leads to
19. Architect _____ Saarinen
20. Dir. from Okla. City to Tulsa: Init.
21. Many, many moons
22. Frightened
24. Crusader's adversary
27. Taken_____ (surprised)
28. Person pushing a bogus cure or treatment
32. Removes, as a brooch
35. "____ we there yet?"
36. Buzzer
37. Flies high
38. 1/6 of a fluid ounce: Abbr.
39. Tim of *Home Improvement*
41. Cause of inflation?
42. Charge
43. Cleric
44. Famed English explorer and privateer
48. Gift of the Magi
49. Tangle up
53. Slender and elegant
55. Regrettable
56. Luau souvenir
57. Former Yugoslav leader
58. Common unit of currency
62. Microwave, e.g.
63. Locket shape
64. Nun's outfit
65. *Star* _____
66. Like the taste of venison
67. Leaves out

DOWN

1. Acid neutralizers
2. Sports venue
3. More upscale
4. Big deal
5. Deighton or Berman
6. Elegant typeface
7. Like ____ of bricks
8. Column's counterpart
9. Well-founded
10. Illuminating comment (from the French)
11. Fragile
12. When repeated, a vitamin B deficiency
13. Footless animal
18. Exploits
23. Web site help, briefly
25. Mideast chief: Var.
26. Millennium divs.: Abbr.
27. Modern Maturity org.
29. Scoped out, as part of planning a heist
30. So-so grades
31. Clark of the *Daily Planet*
32. American mil. branch: Init.
33. Black, in Bordeaux
34. Measurable factor
38. New Age pianist John _____
39. Synagogue chests
40. Security for a debt
42. Andiron
43. Black-and-white zoo favorite
45. Hose
46. Old PC screen initials
47. "For sure!"
50. Claim that one was elsewhere when the crime was committed
51. Kindled anew
52. Cheerful tunes
53. Pack away
54. _____ *Las Vegas* (Presley flick)
55. Hit hard
59. Eggs, in old Rome
60. Density symbol
61. Emeril exclamation

№7 DUCK SOUP

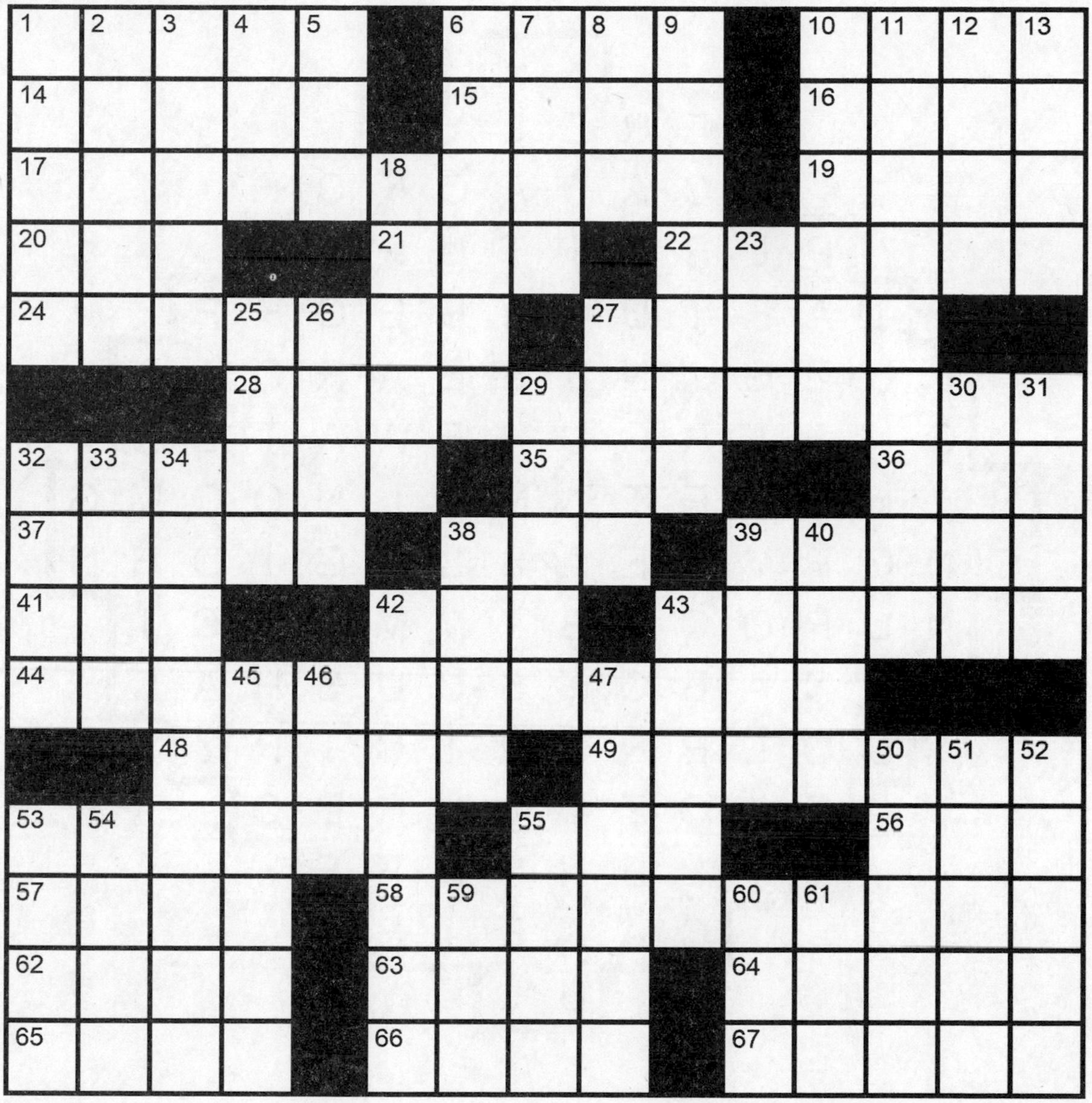

1960S TRIVIA CHALLENGE

Can you name this 1963 movie starring Elizabeth Taylor and Richard Burton as famous historical figures that was the highest-grossing film of that year?

Name the popular sketch comedy TV series that debuted in January of 1968 that made use of a psychedelically painted "Joke Wall" that had open doors behind which cast members and guests would appear and crack jokes.

№2 ROUND THINGS

					X	P							
			E	R	E	L	Y	K					
			I	C	A	D	A	O	K	C			
		P	L	R	S	I	T	U	P	L	U		
	T	A	E	T	U	S	E	B	E	O	R	P	
	C	U	Z	G	I	N	K	B	E	A	R	O	I	A
	O	N	Z	A	R	G	U	H	F	W	A	T	L	N
B	I	H	I	B	E	T	W	M	I	L	N	O	O	M	G
Q	N	G	P	V	T	E	A	B	L	P	G	I	D	H	N
	N	U	R	O	O	R	B	I	M	M	E	I	C	I
	V	O	N	A	B	O	T	S	U	U	S	H	A	K
		D	O	L	P	R	L	R	I	C	T	R	Z
		E	L	O	E	D	L	U	R	D	O
		T	L	E	N	S	A	F	F
		C	A	K	E	I	B
			B	L

BAGEL	DOUGHNUT	LOOP	PLATE
BALL	DRAIN	MARBLE	PUCK
BALLOON	DRUM	MOON	RING
BUTTON	EARTH	ORANGE	SUN
CAKE	FRISBEE	PEA	TIRE
COIN	GRAPE	PEAR	TORTILLA
DISCUS	LENS	PIE	WHEEL
DISK	LIFEBUOY	PIZZA	

№3 PICNIC GET-TOGETHERS

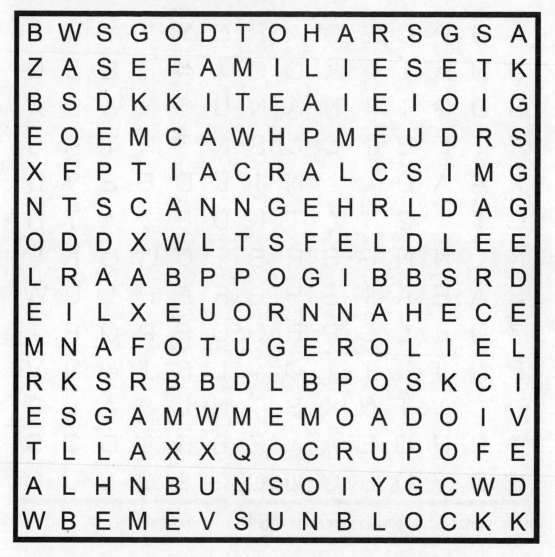

```
B W S G O D T O H A R S G S A
Z A S E F A M I L I E S E T K
B S D K K I T E A I E I O I G
E O E M C A W H P M F U D R S
X F P T I A C R A L C S I M G
N T S C A N N G E H R L D A G
O D D X W L T S F E L D L E E
L R A A B P P O G I B B S R D
E I L X E U O R N N A H E C E
M N A F O T U G E R O L I E L
R K S R B B D L B P O S K C I
E S G A M W M E M O A D O I V
T L L A X X Q O C R U P O F E
A L H N B U N S O I Y G C W D
W B E M E V S U N B L O C K K
```

BADMINTON
BARBEQUE
BEER
BOOM BOX
BUNS
CAKES
COOKIES
COOLER

DEVILED EGGS
FAMILIES
GAMES
GRILLING
GROUP SELFIES
HAMBURGERS
HOT DOGS
ICE CREAM

ICED TEA
KIDS
KITE
LAWN CHAIR
PAPER PLATES
PIES
SALADS
SNACKS

SOFT DRINKS
SONGS
SUN BLOCK
TOUCH FOOTBALL
WATERMELON

№4 ON THE DIAGONAL

A	H	P	C	S	D	A	F	C	Y	Y	Y	B	L
U	N	A	I	T	K	G	C	I	X	R	E	Z	U
S	D	G	T	T	N	A	N	U	G	N	W	P	X
X	T	E	U	I	C	C	S	N	T	N	T	A	S
X	A	A	D	L	L	H	I	K	D	E	E	Y	D
G	T	I	G	I	A	T	K	D	E	J	A	T	H
N	L	N	N	G	S	R	E	T	C	W	O	F	E
S	A	E	A	I	E	P	E	R	E	P	L	U	W
Z	D	E	L	C	P	R	O	D	P	P	Q	F	T
P	N	J	L	I	I	O	I	L	R	I	O	N	V
U	L	I	T	N	K	S	I	N	L	E	A	L	F
O	N	H	G	E	A	N	E	B	G	L	D	Q	S
E	D	V	D	B	G	U	O	G	S	Q	L	U	O

In this word search, all the key words have a kinship with the word "diagonal" and can only be found on the diagonals of the grid.

ACUTE	CANT	OBLIQUE	SLOPE
ANGULAR	CROOKED	PITCH	STAGGERING
ASKEW	INCLINED	RECLINE	TEETERING
ATILT	LEAN	SIDEWAYS	TIPPED
AWRY	LISTING	SLANT	TOPPLING
BENT	LOPSIDED	SLIDING	

№5 RED THINGS

```
N D O T N E I M I P A A O O G
R O M C N N A L E O P F S Y U
U Q L I M I S T O P S I G N B
B A W E R Z W C L B M R I U Y
Y T V G M S A E X Y S E F A D
R V N Y R R E B W A R T S D A
A A U A D H E T I E N R E O L
S O S I E S U T O Q K U E R R
G C N P U R T B A M D C H H M
H A K N B E I K A W A K I A C
L H S E S E I F Q R G T R R Y
L E E N Z R R N N K B S O Z B
T T I I P V E R M I L I O N R
S O U A O Q A B Y H S I D A R
P A P P P B R E P P E P T O H
```

APPLE	FIRE ANT	POINSETTIA	STRAWBERRY
BARN	FIRE TRUCK	RADISH	SUNSET
BEETS	HOT PEPPER	RASPBERRY	TOMATO
BRICK	LADYBUG	RHUBARB	VERMILION
CARDINAL	LOBSTER	ROSE	WATERMELON
CHERRY	MARS	RUBY	WINE
CLAY	PAPRIKA	SANGRIA	
FIGS	PIMIENTO	STOP SIGN	

№6 CHRISTMAS TREES

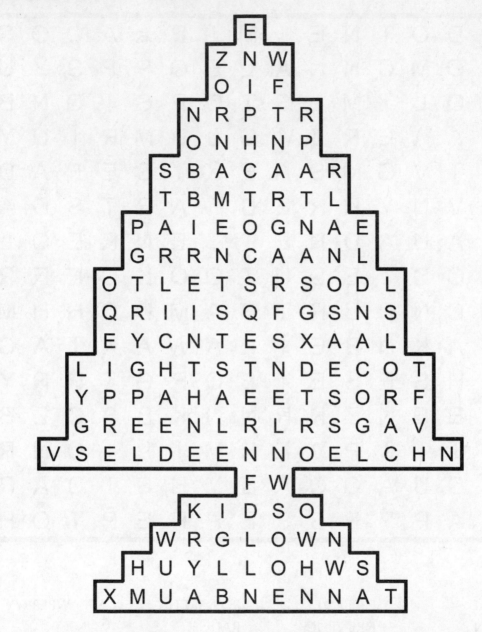

```
                    E
                  Z N W
                O I F
              N R P T R
            O N H N P
          S B A C A A R
        T B M T R T L
      P A I E O G N A E
    G R R N C A A N L
  O T L E T S R S O D L
  Q R I I S Q F G S N S
  E Y C N T E S X A A L
L I G H T S T N D E C O T
Y P P A H A E E T S O R F
G R E E N L R L R S G A V
V S E L D E E N N O E L C H N
              F W
            K I D S O
          W R G L O W N
        H U Y L L O H W S
      X M U A B N E N N A T
```

CANDLE	GREEN	ORNAMENTS	STAND
CAROLS	HAPPY	PRESENTS	STAR
FIR	HOLLY	RIBBON	TALL
FRAGRANT	KIDS	SANTA	TANNENBAUM
FROST	LIGHTS	SCOTCH PINE	TINSEL
GLITTER	NEEDLES	SEASONAL	TRIM
GLOW	NOEL	SNOW	

№7 SECOND CITY—A COUNTRY'S SECOND-LARGEST CITY BY POPULATION

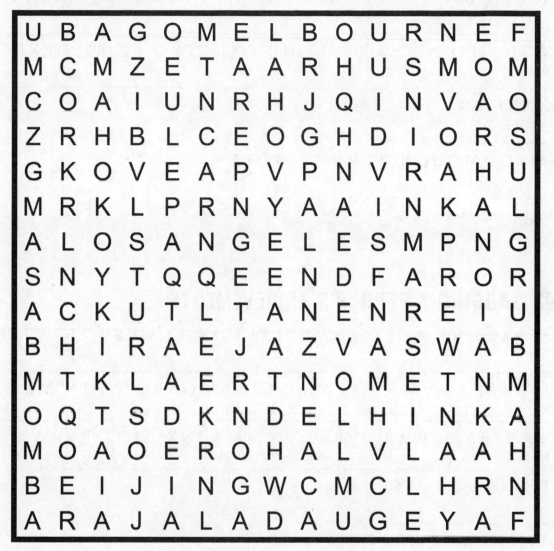

```
U B A G O M E L B O U R N E F
M C M Z E T A A R H U S M O M
C O A I U N R H J Q I N V A O
Z R H B L C E O G H D I O R S
G K O V E A P V P N V R A H U
M R K L P R N Y A A I N K A L
A L O S A N G E L E S M P N G
S N Y T Q Q E E N D F A R O R
A C K U T L T A N E N R E I U
B H I R A E J A Z V A S W A B
M T K L A E R T N O M E T N M
O Q T S D K N D E L H I N K A
M O A O E R O H A L V L A A H
B E I J I N G W C M C L H R N
A R A J A L A D A U G E Y A F
```

AARHUS, denmark
ANKARA, turkey
ANTWERP, belgium
BARCELONA, spain
BEIJING, china
BERGEN, norway
BIRMINGHAM, u.k.
CORK, ireland
DELHI, india

EL ALTO, bolivia
FEZ, morocco
GENEVA, switzerland
GRAZ, austria
GUADALAJARA, mexico
HAMBURG, germany
HANOI, vietnam
KRAKOW, poland

LAHORE, pakistan
LOS ANGELES, u.s.a.
MARSEILLE, france
MELBOURNE, australia
MILAN, italy
MOMBASA, kenya
MONTREAL, canada
MOSUL, iraq
ORAN, algeria

PORTO, portugal
QUITO, ecuador
RIO DE JANEIRO, brazil
ROTTERDAM, netherlands
TEL AVIV, israel
YOKOHAMA, japan

№2 GET THE JOB DONE

IXGIQGJBMJQ MTT PXFB JLXFELJA FCXG JLQ SXBH MJ

_____

LMGU. JLQ AFG'A BMPA UX GXJ OFBG FGJRT OBXFELJ

_____

JX NXIFA.

_____

—MTQDMGUQB EBMLMV OQTT

_____

HINTS (SEE PAGE 138): 27, 35, 40

№3 GAUGING A PERSON'S ACHIEVEMENTS

BZSSXBB RB AJ EX OXMBZLXK UJA BJ OZSV EH AVX

_____

GJBRARJU AVMA JUX VMB LXMSVXK RU WRTX MB EH

_____

AVX JEBAMSWXB PVRSV VX VMB JNXLSJOX PVRWX

_____

ALHRUI AJ BZSSXXK.

_____

—EJJFXL A. PMBVRUIAJU

_____

HINTS (SEE PAGE 138): 4, 17, 23

№4 USE IT OR LOSE IT

WFHE FNKCK SFHR UWKNKX, QPCXF IHKXK WCK

_____

GNFWCD SFHR KCPOEPCWHE; XLXE KH UHXK WEPJCWHE

_____

KPG CAX LWOHF HS CAX RWEU.

_____

—IXHEPFUH UP LWEJW

_____

HINTS (SEE PAGE 138): 5, 24, 32

№5 REALLY HITTING IT OFF

DLANQDI ONL PHIO ULFTVNOSBF SATLXUINTDI QAL

_____

ONHIL TX MNTRN ONLAL TI PBRN QVALLPLXO, PBRN

_____

UTIDBOQOTHX, QXU ELO PHAL DLAIHXQF FTZTXV.

_____

—VLHAVL LFTHO

_____

HINTS (SEE PAGE 138): 7, 13, 34

№6 DEALING WITH OUR LIMITATIONS

PK DSVF CK DUBPSVFB UB CKP UC POF GKIFJ KN

_____

OLDSCB; ELP NJKD POFUJ FJJKJB SCR DUBPSVFB POF

_____

IUBF SCR MKKR TFSJC IUBRKD NKJ POF NLPLJF.

_____

—GTLPSJZO

_____

HINTS (SEE PAGE 138): 6, 12 , 37

№7 EVERYONE'S BIG POTENTIAL

JLJIR XIJFN SIJFP HJXTAB MTNV F SIJFPJI. FCMFRB

_____

IJPJPHJI, RDE VFLJ MTNVTA RDE NVJ BNIJAXNV, NVJ

_____

KFNTJAUJ, FAS NVJ KFBBTDA ND IJFUV WDI NVJ

_____

BNFIB ND UVFAXJ NVJ MDICS.

_____

—VFIITJN NEHPFA

_____

HINTS (SEE PAGE 138): 1, 22, 30

SUDOKU

SUDOKU №2

	7			8				
2	3	9					1	
6					9	2		
		7	8				2	4
			5		4			
1	9				2	7		
		5	9					1
	8					4	5	2
				5			6	

SUDOKU №3

						1		
7					5		2	
4		8		1		3	5	6
		1		7				
6			5	2	4			8
				6		5		
1	3	5		9		6		7
	4		6					5
		2						

SUDOKU №4

		4	5	8	6			
2				4		5		8
					1		4	
8		1		2	5			
			7	6		8		2
	3		4					
9		2		1				5
			8	9	7	1		

SUDOKU №5

1						3	9	
9	3	5			8			2
		6			1			8
	1			5		9		
5								1
		9		2			6	
8			7			5		
6			3			1	4	9
	5	1						3

SUDOKU №6

	8	7			2			
	6		3		1			2
	2			7	6	8		
	7	5			9			
			4			5	2	
		3	2	9			7	
4			7		3		5	
			6			2	3	

SUDOKU №7

2		8	7	1				
	4			3			9	1
				5				
	2		1					6
	7	6				1	4	
5				3		2		
			9					
4	6		2			5		
			6	7	9		3	

CALCUDOKU

CALCUDOKU №2

4 :	5+		2 :
	1-		
1-		3×	
	1-		4

CALCUDOKU №3

10×		4×	6+	
0-	4		0-	
		15×		20×
2 :				
8+		2-		1

CALCUDOKU №4

7+		**3-**		**1**
12+		**2 :**		**3**
	2×	**12+**		**10×**
2×			**8+**	
	5			**4**

CALCUDOKU №5

2	**12+**		**8×**	**3**	**5**
9+		**9+**		**8+**	
			15×		**6×**
7+	**18×**			**10×**	
	12×		**6×**		**6+**
5		**2**		**6**	

CALCUDOKU №6

3+		20×	30×		18×
3	2		12+		
6	3×				20×
5×	72×	5+		6+	
			13+		6+
20×					

CALCUDOKU №7

3	2	12×	20×		
6+	4			10+	18×
	8+	9+	5		
8+				2×	
	15+		7+		6+
4			8+		

FUTOSHIKI №2

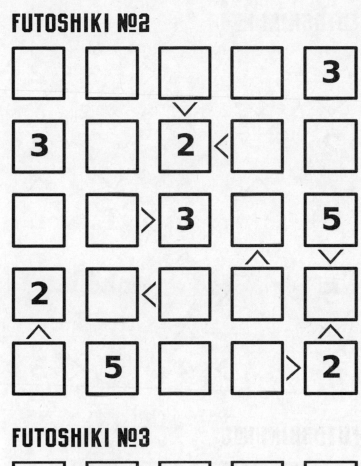

FUTOSHIKI №3

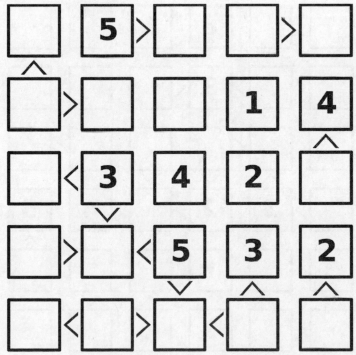

FUTOSHIKI №4

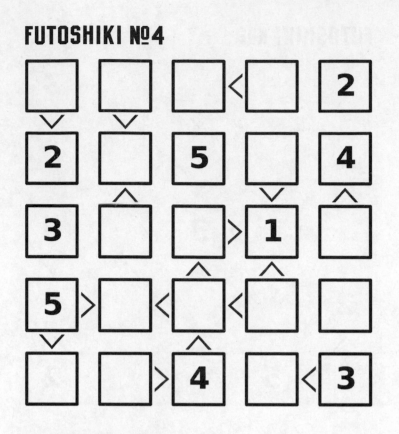

FUTOSHIKI №5

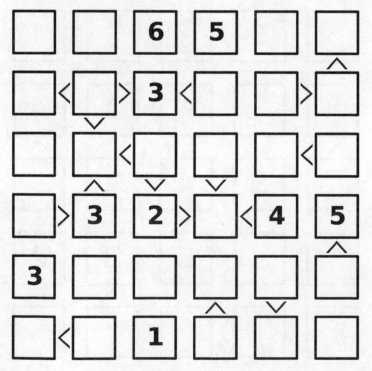

FUTOSHIKI №6

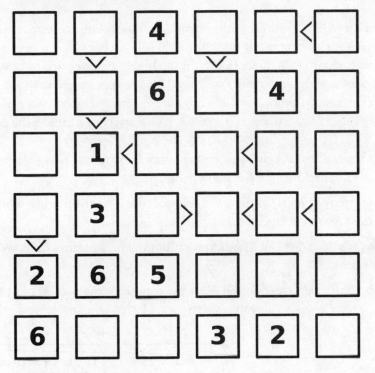

FUTOSHIKI №7

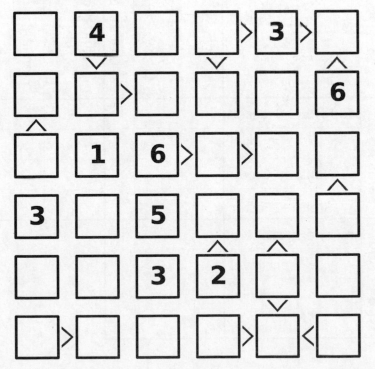

№ 2 CHECKING OUT HOUSES FOR SALE

Grandview Heights is a well-established residential neighborhood with an eclectic mix of single-family houses. Janelle and Joe are looking to buy into the neighborhood because it is close to well-respected schools and they have young children. So, this warm spring day, they decided to drive through the neighborhood to check out four houses currently advertised for sale that caught their eye in their review of listings. Using the clues set out below, see if you can put together each of the four houses they are looking at today, that house's style of construction, and the real estate agency handling the property.

1. Neither of the houses on Elm Street that they are looking at is being marketed by RE/PRO, nor is either mid-century modern in design.

2. The John Jansten Group is handling the colonial that is on the market, while Smith & Foster doesn't represent the sellers of the split-level house.

3. The house for sale at 1413 W. 83rd Terrace is not the mid-century modern nor a craftsman-style house.

4. Neither Top-Notch Houses nor RE/PRO is the realtor for the owners of 8196 Upton St.; and the Jansten Group isn't involved in the sale of 7708 Elm St.

		Address				Type of House			
		7417 Elm St.	7708 Elm St.	1413 W. 83rd Terr.	8196 Upton St.	mid-cent. modern	split-level	colonial	craftsman
Sales Agent	Top-Notch Houses								
	RE/PRO								
	Jansten Group								
	Smith & Foster								
Type of House	mid-cent. modern								
	split-level								
	colonial								
	craftsman								

№3 PRESEASON BASKETBALL TOURNAMENT

It is early November, and the Metro City Arena will be hosting a preseason college basketball tournament this weekend featuring four teams from around the region. To set the stage for the tournament, see whether you can link, from the clues set out below, each college represented in the tournament with the nickname for its team and the main pretournament buzz about its team.

1. The colleges booked for the tournament include Bucolic College, the school whose team is nicknamed the Chieftains, and the school whose team has just recruited a top-ranked point guard as a freshman.

2. Neither Hamilton-Witt U. nor Upland State has just recruited a star point guard or has just welcomed a new coach to the team.

3. Midcentral U.'s team is not nicknamed the Titans or Bulldogs; and the team with the 7'2" center is not the Chieftains or the Titans.

4. Hamilton-Witt's team is not the one that has all its starters from last season returning this year.

		Nickname				Buzz			
		Bulldogs	Chieftains	Titans	Warriors	7'2" center	new coach	freshman guard	returning starters
College	Bucolic College								
College	Hamilton-Witt								
College	Midcentral U.								
College	Upland State								
Buzz	7'2" center								
Buzz	new coach								
Buzz	freshman guard								
Buzz	returning starters								

№4 DOG SHOW WINNERS

The Middletown Kennel Club just wrapped up proceedings at its annual dog show and is pleased with its success. Hundreds of dogs competed, and the winners are among best of their breeds nationwide. First-through fourth-place ribbons were awarded in the Best In Show competition, and the clues below provide a little information on these four ribbon winners. See whether you can take these bits of information and piece together a fuller picture of the winning dogs and their breeds.

1. The winning dogs included Blarney Tom, the English springer spaniel, and the dog awarded the yellow ribbon for coming in third.

2. Pamela's J. K. is not the wire fox terrier who won a ribbon and neither took the blue ribbon (first place) nor finished in third place.

3. Gentle Boomer is not a bichon frise, and Dashing Reggie is not a Pekingese.

4. Dashing Reggie finished better than Gentle Boomer; Blarney Tom didn't grab the blue ribbon.

5. The wire fox terrier didn't take the red ribbon for coming in second, and Dashing Reggie is not a bichon frise.

		Breed				Ribbon Won			
		bichon frise	springer	terrier	Pekingese	blue (1st place)	red (2nd place)	yellow (3rd place)	white (4th place)
Dog	Blarney Tom								
	Dashing Reggie								
	Gentle Boomer								
	Pamela's J. K.								
Ribbon Won	blue (1st place)								
	red (2nd place)								
	yellow (3rd place)								
	white (4th place)								

№5 STRING QUARTET

The four members of the Metro City String Quartet recently were interviewed for a profile in the Metro City *Gazette-Star*. As part of the interview, the *Gazette-Star* reporter asked each member whom his or her favorite composer for string quartets was. Use the hints provided by the clues below to figure out for each member of the ensemble which instrument the person plays and which great composer is his or her fav.

1. Neither of the male members of the ensemble chose Mozart or Debussy as their favorite string quartet composer.

2. Stella does not play a violin, and Suzanne does not play the viola (nor does she consider Debussy her favorite string quartet composer).

3. The group's cellist (who is not Stan or Stella) doesn't rank Schubert as the No. 1 composer for string quartets.

4. Neither Stan nor the quartet's second violin is the big Beethoven fan among the four.

		Instrument				Composer			
		first violin	second violin	viola	cello	Beethoven	Debussy	Mozart	Schubert
Member	Sigmund								
	Stan								
	Stella								
	Suzanne								
Composer	Beethoven								
	Debussy								
	Mozart								
	Schubert								

№ 6 BEER TASTING

One of the area's largest drafthouses has just held a craft beer tasting competition. The dozens of beers that entered the contest were graded on aroma, appearance, flavor, body, and overall appeal. Your challenge is to use the clues below to determine the ratings of the four beers that ended up with the top ratings (on a scale of 1.0 to 10) in the competition, along with the type of beer each of these winners was.

1. The Bridgestone beer that won accolades is not a pilsner; the Denmont Brewing entry with a high rating is not an IPA; and the lauded Old Ralston entry is not a wheat beer.

2. The pale ale favorite was not ranked .3 points higher than another of the four preferred beers.

3. Neither the Klein's Bierwerks nor Old Ralston winner received a rating of 8.5 or 8.8.

4. The beer with the 8.5 rating is not the IPA or the pilsner, and the IPA didn't receive an 8.8 rating.

5. The Klein's entry is a pale ale; it didn't get an 8.2 rating.

		Type of Beer				Rating			
		IPA	pale ale	pilsner	wheat	8.2	8.5	8.8	9.0
Beer Brand	Bridgestone								
	Denmont Brewing								
	Klein's Bierwerks								
	Old Ralston								
Rating	8.2								
	8.5								
	8.8								
	9.0								

CHAPTER 3
MEDIUM PUZZLES

CROSSWORD

ACROSS

1. How some stocks are sold
6. Identical
10. Wild mountain goat
14. Arrange (cloth) around or over something
15. Clothes presser
16. Approach
17. Really steamed
19. Greek salad ingredient
20. Iridescent gem
21. MIT pt.
22. Impudent
23. Piano-like instrument that produces bell-sounding notes
25. Family folk
26. Acting with pride and confidence
32. Farm land unit
35. Wrestles with a decision (with "over")
36. What George Washington couldn't tell
37. Morocco's capital
39. A deadly sin
40. Southwestern spread owner
42. Famed Spanish muralist
43. Relaxing
46. State south of Wash.
47. Contaminated
52. Pebble, e.g.
55. Combine
57. Continental coin
58. Metered vehicle
59. Getting close to the bottom of the barrel
61. Many a golf tournament
62. *Tosca* tune
63. Come up
64. Twinge
65. NFL pt.
66. Flutist

DOWN

1. Impromptu
2. Figure of speech
3. Vatican-related
4. Waldorf salad ingredient
5. King, in Portugal
6. Use a blinker
7. Venus de Milo's lack
8. Castle defense
9. Conclude
10. Very childish
11. Spelling contests
12. Vittles
13. Certain diagnostic test
18. Naldi of old films
22. Portent
24. Scand. country
25. Granny or half hitch
27. Skewered meat (from the Arabic)
28. Food store chain initials
29. Bleu shade
30. Out of concern that
31. WWII landing craft
32. Part of a court game name
33. Military version of POTUS
34. Calculation, estimation
36. Biblical boat
37. Philosopher Descartes
38. So. Amer. country
41. Add to the payroll
42. Hit the slopes
44. Like some modern music
45. Colombian city
48. Old-time actress Pola
49. Garden bulb
50. Jagged, as a leaf's edge
51. Widow's portion, under common law
52. "Cut that out!"
53. Spanish appetizer
54. Yoked beasts
55. Aqua _____ (bottled water brand)
56. Words after sleep
59. Operated
60. Brief time out?

№8 USE YOUR LEGS

THINK ABOUT IT

The *International Journal of Geriatric Psychiatry* in 2019 published the results of studies that concluded that the more regularly adults aged 50 and over played puzzles such as crosswords and Sudoku, the better their brain functions were. The researchers determined these puzzlers did better across a range of tasks involving memory, attention, and reasoning. The improvements were particularly clear in the speed and accuracy of performance.

ACROSS

1. Diamond weight unit
6. Seville's land
11. "Well, lah-de-___!"
14. Garlicky sauce
15. Electrical pioneer
16. That, in Seville
17. "I've looked and looked, but I can't find my kiwis and mangos," Tom cried _____
19. Chinese food general
20. Hurricane's center
21. Wigwam relative
22. Say "@#$%!"
24. Gas station abbr.
25. Explosive initials
27. Largest of seven
28. Gardener's tool
31. "He's been my doctor for many years, so I don't mind if he's running late," Tom said _____
33. Fertile soil
34. Carrier to Copenhagen
35. "Give that ____ cigar!"
36. "Let's just take it easy and dig into that candy," Tom murmured _____
38. "To get her attention, I'll put it all in a very short letter," Tom said _____
41. Earth goddess
42. The "p" in mpg
43. Azure
44. "Look, we should keep trying because I just know it's impossible to lose every game," Tom argued _____
47. Considers, holds
48. Missouri River native
49. Atlanta-to-Miami dir.
50. Mas' mates
51. _____ Gras
53. Less risky
55. Best guess: Abbr.
58. Shade tree
59. "I foresee that the sun will come up in the east tomorrow," Tom ventured _____
62. Vardalos or Peeples
63. More reasonable
64. Downloaded novel
65. ___ Diego, CA
66. Unique persons
67. *The Divine Comedy* poet

DOWN

1. Bistro
2. Well-ventilated
3. Libertine
4. Ring great
5. Nervous giggle
6. Big first for a baby
7. Coins formerly used in Seville
8. Expression of approval
9. Under the weather
10. Thumbs-down votes
11. Loathsome
12. Attack
13. "Hip hip" follower
18. Chair part
23. Aspirants, slangily
24. Let go
26. Indonesian island
28. Fat letters
29. Black bird
30. Famous Australian golfer
31. Foot the bill
32. Chow down
34. Criticizes severely
37. Uncle, in Seville
38. Marshal under Napoleon
39. Abner's buddy from old radio
40. "You bet"
42. Supplicant
44. Department store section
45. Firenze's land
46. Ancient ascetic
47. Scooted
50. Chest muscle, for short
52. ____ facto
54. Some evergreens
55. Lustrous black
56. Narrow opening
57. Small child
60. Skedaddled
61. Attorneys' org.

№9 TOM SWIFTIES

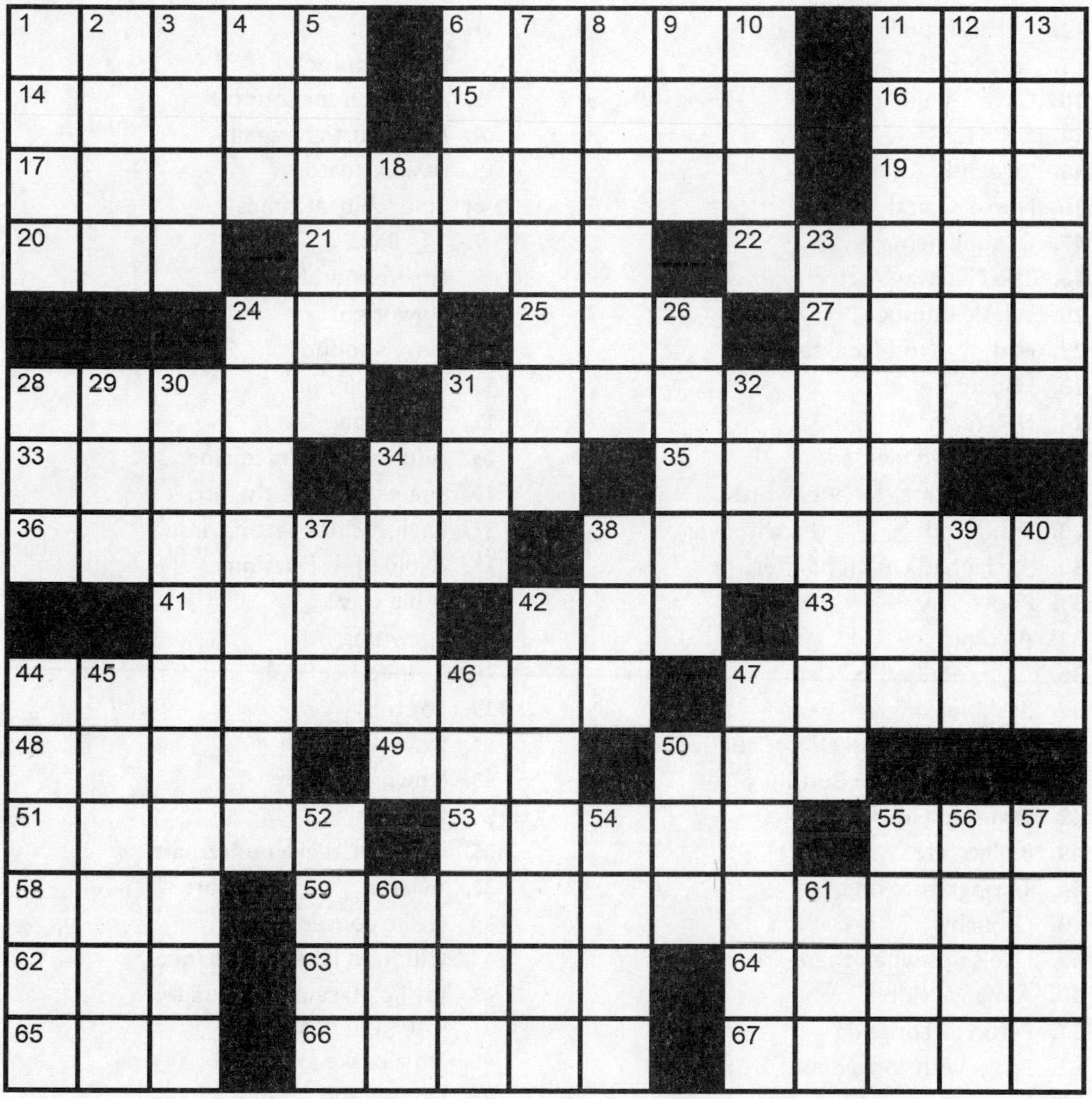

1970S TRIVIA CHALLENGE

Who was the North Carolina senator who chaired the televised U.S. Senate Committee hearings into the Watergate scandal?

What is the name of the Manhattan nightclub that opened in April 1977 and quickly became a center of the disco music and dancing craze then sweeping the country?

ACROSS

1. *Rubáiyát* poet
5. Texas shrine, with "the"
10. Gave a stage signal
14. Grimace
15. Rice dish: Alt. spelling
16. Norse capital
17. Capone nemesis
18. The Gateway Arch city
20. Whole number
22. Mai ___ (rum cocktail)
23. Had a bite
24. NFL team
25. Channeled, guided
27. Ten Commandments word
29. Front-end _____ (earthmover)
30. Acclaimed Dutch painter
31. Photo
32. Anxious
36. "___ recall . . ."
37. Backbreaking
39. Suffix with "musket" or "auction"
40. Cosmic order, in Buddhism
42. Order to Fido
43. Bullets, etc.
44. Temperature unit
46. Grouchy
47. Like ships when there are no winds
50. Almanac tidbit
51. Perón or Longoria
52. Suffix with "president" or "proverb"
53. Family helpers from abroad
56. Changes
59. Means of access
60. Genesis garden
61. Foolish
62. Ancient Andean
63. Minus
64. Roman goddess of agriculture
65. Inquires

DOWN

1. All: Prefix
2. Faucet brand
3. Down Under country
4. Makes airtight again
5. Basilica features
6. Pinocchio, at times
7. ___ Baba
8. Northern Italy city
9. Downright
10. Dove's sound
11. Customary
12. Type type
13. Administered medicine
19. Sheets, tablecloths, etc.
21. English clock setting: Init.
25. Avoided distractions
26. "Able was I ___ . . ."
27. Spawning fish
28. Corned beef dish
29. Pot top
31. Down-to-earth
33. Downgrades
34. Beauties
35. Cupid's Greek counterpart
37. Aviator _____ Earhart
38. Gallic goose
41. Old food label figure: Init.
43. Idyllic place of tranquility, or region of Greece
45. Do a brake job
46. Upper limit
47. Angled cut
48. Circumvent
49. Is concerned
50. Welds
53. *Green Gables* girl
54. Move the cradle
55. Madrid Mmes.
57. They have clout
58. Rowing blade

№10 DOWN WE GO

1	2	3	4	■	5	6	7	8	9	■	10	11	12	13
14				■	15					■	16			
17				■	18				19					
20				21			■	22			■	23		
■		24				■	25			■	26			
27	28				■	29					■	■	■	■
30				■	31			■	32			33	34	35
36			■	37			■	38			■	39		
40			41			■	42			■	43			
■	■	■	44			45		■	46				■	■
47	48	49			■			50				■	■	■
51			■	52			■	53				■	54	55
56			57			■	58			■	59			
60			■	61						■	62			
63			■	64						■	65			

DID YOU KNOW?

According to the British Library, Robert Cawdrey's *Table Alphabeticall*, published in 1604, was the first single-language English dictionary ever published. It lists approximately 3,000 words, defining each one with a simple and brief description. Today, the *Oxford English Dictionary* has over 600,000 entries.

ACROSS

1. Outlaws
5. Clubs or spades
9. Triumphs over
14. Seven U.S. presidents were born here
15. Europe's highest volcano
16. Data fed to a computer
17. This is low for a sports car
20. _____ and the Night Visitors (Menotti opera)
21. Supermodel stances
22. Owing
23. "O" preceders in a children's song
25. Remove from a manuscript, in editing lingo
27. Highway barrier
32. Golf resort near Miami
35. High regard
36. Doze (with "off")
38. Sch. with generals as alums
39. Sylvester, to Tweety
40. Burdened (with)
43. Drollery
44. Long, long time
46. ___-disant (self-styled)
47. Calm and collected
49. Article of faith
51. Container for items like hooks and lures
53. Have the nerve
55. Thunderbirds org.
56. 180° from NNW
58. Fable man of old
61. Art-class subjects
65. Doctor who specializes in treating glandular conditions
68. Church donation
69. Anger, with "up"
70. Other
71. Rose
72. Doe's mate
73. Swill

DOWN

1. East Coast Florida town, briefly
2. Attention-seeking sound
3. Singer Simone
4. "Take that!"
5. Pulpit talk: Abbr.
6. Perfect world
7. Facts and figures, succinctly
8. License plates, informally
9. Prejudiced
10. Ltr. holder
11. Wispy construction
12. Ballet attire
13. Eyelid ailment
18. Skips over in pronunciation
19. Cabernet, e.g.
24. Bombeck and others
26. Gehrig or Costello
27. Imply
28. Grammarian's concern
29. Handled
30. Asian country
31. Texter's chuckle
33. Acid type
34. Paint variety
37. Escritoires
41. Period
42. Presidential middle name
45. Vast amount
48. Safe places
50. Found by investigation
52. Dome-like structure
54. Poetic contraction
56. Adjusts, as a clock
57. Hissy fit
59. "Dear" ones
60. See 64 Down
62. Pickle flavoring
63. Canadian gas brand
64. With 60 Down, phrase meaning "Go faster, driver!"
66. "Well, lookee here!"
67. Journey segment

№11 ALL ON THE LINE

1	2	3	4	■	5	6	7	8	■	9	10	11	12	13
14				■	15				■	16				
17				18					19					
20				■		21					■	22		
■	■		23		24		■		25		26		■	■
27	28	29					30	31	■	32			33	34
35						■	36		37	■	38			
39			■	40		41				42	■	43		
44			45		46		■	47		48				
49				50	■	51		52						
■		53			54		■	55				■	■	■
56	57		■	58		59	60		■	61		62	63	64
65			66						67					
68				■	69				■	70				
71					■	72			■	73				

THINK ABOUT IT

Don't neglect to include socialization as an important part of your brain health exercise regimen. Social activity is not only important emotionally, but it has a cognitive aspect to it as well. When you are in a social situation, you are exercising your cognitive resources to engage in verbal volleying, remembering names, following the agenda if the event is a structured one, and so on.

ACROSS

1. Borscht vegetable
5. Tiny, in Troon
8. Comparable, distance-wise
13. Legal rights org.
14. Blacken on a grill
15. Myanmar, once
16. EAGLE
18. Converse
19. Observing Ramadan
21. Actress Falco
22. Adlai's 1956 running mate
25. DOVE
27. Bolted
29. Religious schs.
30. The Monkees' "___ Believer"
31. Opening on Broadway?
35. Aquarium fish
38. CRANE
42. Electrical weapon
43. Song for two
44. Here, in France
45. Lippo Lippi and Angelico
47. Sound system
50. CARDINAL
55. Lulus
56. "The night ____ thousand eyes"
57. Seltzer maker
59. Cream of the crop
61. PIGEON
65. Healing plants
66. Ski lift
67. Put on board
68. Inclines
69. Word part: Abbr.
70. "____ we forget"

DOWN

1. Capture
2. *Foucault's Pendulum* author
3. Kay follower
4. Nursery rhyme seat
5. Quick drinks
6. Andretti or Puzo
7. *Gladiator* setting
8. Stomach muscles, briefly
9. All guys from Krypton, presumably
10. Legendary screen dancer
11. At full speed
12. Did a fall chore
14. Shares an email with, briefly
17. Encl. with a MS.
20. Modern navig. tool
22. Decree
23. Girl Scout cookie type
24. Medical procedure
26. Texas pol O'Rourke
28. Women's patriotic org.
32. Something to chew on
33. Horned Frogs' sch.
34. Mineral suffix
36. Potato gadget
37. Parting word for Pablo
39. Like saws
40. ____ II (razor model discontinued in 2022)
41. Part of TGIF
46. ___ Na Na
48. Choo-choo's sound
49. Sign up
50. Deal from the bottom of the deck
51. Oscar-winning Berry
52. Athletic contests
53. "The Sheik of _____" (Jazz Age tune)
54. Nose-related
58. Norse war god
60. Tee preceder
62. Abu Dhabi's land, for short
63. Parts of finan. portfolios
64. Worked (up)

№12 A FLOCK OF CLUES

1980S TRIVIA CHALLENGE

What is the name of this 3-D combination puzzle invented by a Hungarian professor that became a best-selling toy in the early 1980s and is still popular even today?

Who were the unsuccessful candidates for president and vice president in 1984 who lost to the Ronald Reagan/George Bush ticket?

ACROSS

1. Soliloquy start
5. Amber or umber
10. Israeli port
14. Taj Mahal site
15. Pitch
16. Active sort
17. Cheap statue just depicting a guy?
19. Clothes, informally
20. Do a slow burn
21. Choir voice
23. "Hogwash!"
24. 1998 National League MVP
26. Aid in committing a crime
28. U.S. mil. medal
31. King's 65-watt floods?
36. _____ Frome
38. Elevator inventor
39. Joint ailment
40. Brothers who made *Fargo*
41. ____ Tin Tin
42. Traveler's pathway
43. Prayer ender
44. After-Christmas event
45. Follow
46. Put lifts in one's shoes?
49. Particularly: Abbr.
50. "Aha!"
51. Shore bird
53. Fish feature
55. Dresden's river
58. *Citizen Kane*'s real-life model
62. Brainchild
64. Terse report about the French bakery not making sufficient quiches for its customers today?
66. Befuddled
67. Early anesthetic
68. Letter before kappa
69. ". . . or ___!"
70. Lyon's river
71. Headliner

DOWN

1. Bugler's evening call
2. Leer
3. Highlands hillside
4. Wests' opposites
5. Cracker topper
6. Not 'neath
7. Dalai ____
8. Elliptical
9. Avis availabilities
10. Toss in
11. Place for trials
12. Change (decor)
13. Formerly, formerly
18. Rose stickers
22. ___-Wan Kenobi
25. Ancient meeting places
27. Exhort
28. Joltless joe
29. Leaf opening
30. Impudence
32. Leaning
33. Straight, geometrically
34. *Swan Lake* costumes
35. Precipitous
37. Queen _____ lace
42. Air-conditioning when it's a hot day, maybe
44. Peanut processing gizmo
47. Kickoff aid
48. Pakistan's second-largest city
52. _____ lazuli
53. Carpentry tool
54. Fan favorite
56. Shower alternative
57. Bounce back, in a way
59. Melee
60. ____ precedent
61. Boris Godunov, for one
63. Ended a fast
65. *Jeopardy!* host Jennings

№13 THE SPIRIT OF WILLIAM SPOONER LIVES ON

DID YOU KNOW?

The number zero (0) is a relative latecomer to mathematics—it wasn't until the 1600s that zero came widely to be used. Before then, the concept of zero as a number first took hold in India in the seventh century CE, spread from there to Arabia, and thence to Europe in the thirteenth century.

ACROSS

1. Invitation heading
6. Traveler's stop
11. Short-sleeved pullover
14. Hearing-related
15. Corpulent
16. King: Latin
17. Rig a sporting event by keeping the score down without losing, to beat the spread
19. Choler
20. Auspices: Var.
21. Uno, ___, tres
22. Karaoke prop, for short
23. Alfresco meal
26. Literary word meaning "defames"
28. Knee injury initials
29. Analogous
31. Huffy state
32. Six, in Sicily
33. Word after dish or dust
35. Symbol for an unstressed vowel
38. Easy dupes
40. Anagram for THOSE
42. Get better
43. Trade shows, slangily
45. Legendary storyteller
47. Strong and healthy
48. Arab chieftain
50. Office communication
51. Fifth, e.g.: Abbr.
52. Like smartphones
55. Northern Ireland province
57. Morning times, briefly
58. Hoppy brew: Init.
59. "Beat it!"
60. "Well, ___-di-dah!"
61. Examine (a bunch of stuff) very carefully, looking for something
66. Letters before "Friday!"
67. "_____ Mio" (popular aria for tenors)
68. Part of ICBM
69. Type of IRA, or 30-day mo.
70. Cozy retreats
71. Appears

DOWN

1. Is no longer
2. "Say what?"
3. Chapter in history
4. Poe's talking bird
5. Like a plaintive poem (such as that involving 4 Down)
6. Farm sounds
7. Kimono sash
8. Looks after
9. Prohibits, legally
10. Diminishes
11. Cuts waste, as in a budget
12. Bone-chilling
13. Business VIPs
18. Predicament
23. No longer in
24. Alpine climber's tool
25. 19th-century sailing vessel built for speed
26. Country music?
27. Loaded
30. Scintilla
34. Garden implement
36. Forgo
37. Fiddle with
39. A portion
41. "Thanks _____!"
44. Chip material
46. North Star
49. State of rest
52. Whitman and Disney
53. Public relations concern
54. Aegean island
56. Rock
59. French holy women: Abbr.
62. Deli sandwich initials
63. Arapaho foe
64. Masterpiece
65. Mins. and mins.

№14 BARBERSHOP QUARTET

1	2	3	4	5		6	7	8	9	10		11	12	13
14						15						16		
17				18								19		
		20					21				22			
23	24	25				26			27					
28				29	30		31							
32			33			34		35				36	37	
38		39		40			41		42					
43			44		45			46		47				
	48			49		50				51				
52	53				54		55		56					
57				58		59								
60			61			62				63	64	65		
66			67				68							
69			70				71							

THINK ABOUT IT

Your working memory is a system in the brain that holds information for a short period of time as your brain tackles cognitive tasks at hand. Researchers have found that brain exercises can improve working memory. That is good news for persons interested in maintaining their brain health, as working memory plays a key role in much of our complex everyday cognitive activities.

№8 COOKING UP A STORM

```
Y H C A O P H T T F A W B L
T R I M B E U A Z S R E H E
L S F R E E Z E C B A O A M
M L O P I L D H O T E O S I
J I I G E T A E M L X A R T
L B X R E E S E B M A L F D
L C P I G K D M I O K F B A
E T A N I R A M N G N L J E
T D N D X R K B E R E E F N
A P F T C I C P E N B C O K
R O R S B H E T D A S S I L
G H Y O I S U E B F A S E D
W C I L G A N B R E A D O V
R L L P S T F I S P I H W T
```

BAKE	DEBONE	HEAT	SCRAMBLE
BEAT	DEEP-FRY	KNEAD	SEASON
BLEND	DICE	MARINATE	SHIRR
BOIL	FLAMBE	MIX	SIFT
BREAD	FREEZE	PAN-FRY	STIR
BROIL	FROST	PEEL	TIME
CHILL	GRATE	POACH	TOSS
CHOP	GRILL	ROAST	TRIM
COMBINE	GRIND	SAUTE	WHIP

№9 R GUYS

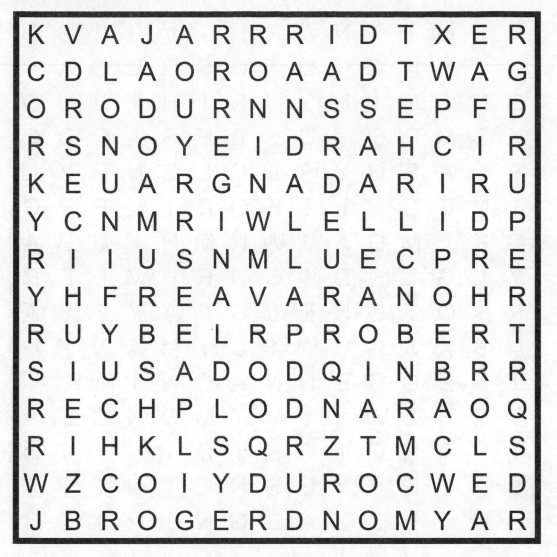

```
K V A J A R R R R I D T X E R
C D L A O R O A A D T W A G
O R O D U R N N S S E P F D
R S N O Y E I D R A H C I R
K E U A R G N A D A R I R U
Y C N M R I W L E L L I D P
R I I U S N M L U E C P R E
Y H F R E A V A R A N O H R
R U Y B E L R P R O B E R T
S I U S A D O D Q I N B R R
R E C H P L O D N A R A O Q
R I H K L S Q R Z T M C L S
W Z C O I Y D U R O C W E D
J B R O G E R D N O M Y A R
```

RAJAV	RAYMOND	RICO	ROLLO
RALPH	REGINALD	ROALD	RONALD
RAMIRO	RENE	ROBERT	RONIN
RAMON	REUBEN	ROBIN	RORY
RANDALL	REX	ROCCO	RUDY
RANDOLPH	RHETT	ROCK	RUFUS
RAPHAEL	RHYS	ROD	RUPERT
RASHID	RICARDO	RODERICK	RYAN
RASMUS	RICHARD	RODNEY	
RAUL	RICKIE	ROGER	

№ 10 EYE-CATCHING

```
H Z G I T N A R B I V B C G O
J C N N G G O T G S R B O A S
G N I N I H S M N I H T L U W
K S M R Q T U H L E G A O D O
F L A S H Y S L C L G N R Y L
T N E C U L I E O D I L F P G
G K L M D A J W R M H X U E A
Y L G L N D I Q U R H M L F R
R I O T O N E L S J A Z Z Y A
E B X S G U W T C I M A N Y D
T N E C S E D N A C N I W L I
T S H O W Y Y V T M Q N C E A
I V T H G I R B I D I V I V N
L F I E R Y E S N E T N I I T
G N I L Z Z A D G N I R A L G
```

AGLOW	DYNAMIC	GLOWING	RICH
ANIMATED	FIERY	INCANDESCENT	SHARP
ARRESTING	FLASHY	INTENSE	SHINING
BOLD	FULGENT	JAZZY	SHOWY
BRIGHT	GAUDY	LIVELY	VIBRANT
BRILLIANT	GLARING	LOUD	VIVID
COLORFUL	GLEAMING	LUCENT	
CORUSCATING	GLITTERY	LUMINOUS	
DAZZLING	GLOSSY	RADIANT	

№11 C SOUNDS

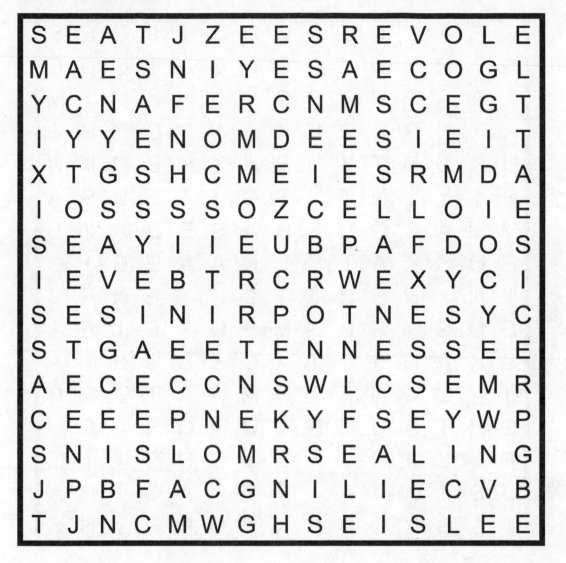

```
S E A T J Z E E S R E V O L E
M A E S N I Y E S A E C O G L
Y C N A F E R C N M S C E G T
I Y Y E N O M D E E S I E I T
X T G S H C M E I E S R M D A
I O S S S S O Z C E L L O I E
S E A Y I I E U B P A F D O S
I E V E B T R C R W E X Y C I
S E S I N I R P O T N E S Y C
S T G A E E T E N N E S S E E
A E C E C C N S W L C S E M R
C E E E P N E K Y F S E Y W P
S N I S L O M R S E A L I N G
J P B F A C G N I L I E C V B
T J N C M W G H S E I S L E E
```

ASSISI

BESIEGE

CEASE

CEILING

CEMENT

CNBC

CONCEIT

CONCEIVE

COURTESY

ELSIE

FANCY

FLEECY

IDIOCY

INSEAM

ITSY-BITSY

ODYSSEY

OVERSEE

PRECIS

PRISSY

RECEDE

RECEIPT

RECEIVE

SCENE

SEALING

SEASHORE

SEAT

SEATTLE

SECANT

SEED MONEY

SEEP

SEESAW

SEIZE

SIESTA

TENNESSEE

№ 12 JAPAN

```
N B A L L I Z D O G I S O E S
W I R F U K O D U S A T O U E
A A A I H S U S S L N K M T M
R T N R H O K K A I D O P H I
U K O D T Y D R H K R B U K N
P I Y Y N T Y S G J A E U B A
M M A O O M E B A S E B A L L
E O S K A T U L N A A E B I O
T N Y N E H J I L K Y E N R B
E O G M S U S M E U X F I E I
S K P N J D T A O K B G N M A
J L O I N F Z N M S A T J E R
E H T A U Q R U C M O S A C U
F S L J R I H S I B U S T I M
U S I W J A I T O T A G I R A
I A S N O B K X N O P P I N S
```

ANIME	ISLANDS	NIPPON	SONY
ARIGATO	JUJITSU	ORIGAMI	SUDOKU
BASEBALL	KABUKI	OSAKA	SUMO
BENTO BOX	KARAOKE	RICE	SUSHI
BONSAI	KIMONO	SAKE	TEMPLE
BULLET TRAIN	KOBE BEEF	SALARYMAN	TEMPURA
GODZILLA	MITSUBISHI	SAMURAI	TOKYO
HOKKAIDO	MT. FUJI	SAYONARA	TOYOTA
HONSHU	NINJA	SHINTO	TSUNAMI

№13 TREES

```
D Y N A G O H A M N E P S A G M
W O L L I W I T R E D O A K L K
O Y O J U L O U T U N T S E H C
D O G W O O D N Y N P U S Y I O
W W S N N Y R R E B K C A H J L
T A G J A O O E S Y A E F B E M
A A L U R K T T R I K D R I C E
M E D N C E H T O O H A A R U H
N N L I U C D U O B M R S C R I
R I H P E T Q B A C M A A H P M
O P Z E P E N S U Y F L C R S A
H G B R S A S Z R D Y N A Y K S
T G K V Y W B R A P P L E P S L
W L Q N O Q E A T I V R O B R A
A Q A O I H I U R T E L P A M B
H B D D C G S F X C Y P R E S S
```

APPLE	CHERRY	HAWTHORN	REDBUD
ARBORVITAE	CHESTNUT	HEMLOCK	SASSAFRAS
ASPEN	COTTONWOOD	HICKORY	SEQUOIA
BALSAM	CRABAPPLE	JUNIPER	SPRUCE
BANYAN	CYPRESS	MAGNOLIA	SYCAMORE
BASSWOOD	DOGWOOD	MAHOGANY	WALNUT
BEECH	ELM	MAPLE	WILLOW
BIRCH	EUCALYPTUS	PALM	
BUTTERNUT	GINKGO	PINE	
CEDAR	HACKBERRY	RED OAK	

№8 A KEY ELEMENT OF OUR BRAIN'S POWER

INTEBNES LA KRS NCXHCM HP KRS RBXNT XLTO, NTO

_____

NK HTUS UHTKNLTA KRS KCHVRLSA HP LKA VNAK NTO

_____

KRS JSNVHTA HP LKA PBKBCS UHTFBSAKA.

_____

—ANXBSI UHISCLOES

_____

HINTS (SEE PAGE 138): 20, 25

№9 THUMBNAIL SKETCHES OF OUR FURRY FRIENDS

VX KFVUKHI OBLHS IEJKT, CYJ SBR ABLHS NJ K

_____

NHLFSJZVFR BLCIEBTJF XJHHBA; NLC CYJ OKC ABLHS

_____

YKQJ CYJ ZKZJ RZKOJ BX FJQJZ IKGVFR K ABZS

_____

CBB ULOY.

_____

—UKZT CAKVF

_____

HINTS (SEE PAGE 138): 21, 28

№10 TRUE LEARNING

FI LKPTFGRCI ROI'G SCE JPTS ACP SFDL TCJJRGGLK

_____

GC JLJCHA CH LDLI SCE JPTS ACP UICE. RG'O XLRIV

_____

FXZL GC KRNNLHLIGRFGL XLGELLI ESFG ACP UICE FIK

_____

ESFG ACP KCI'G.

_____
—FIFGCZL NHFITL

_____
HINTS (SEE PAGE 138): 2, 33

№11 AN ELUSIVE GOAL

BLKKPTVUU PU SPZV L GFNNVEXSR ABPQB, ABVT

_____

KFEUFVO, PU LSALRU GVRJTO JFE CELUK, GFN, PX RJF

_____

APSS UPN OJAT DFPVNSR, WLR LSPCBN FKJT RJF.

_____
—TLNBLTPVS BLANBJETV

_____
HINTS (SEE PAGE 138): 9, 31

№12 WHEN ARMIES COLLIDE

DLP OXDDSPTRPSN RF X FMPVP YT MYVFDXVD MLXYF.

_____

DLP CRVVPK CRSS OP DLP YVP CLY MYVDKYSF DLXD

_____

MLXYF, OYDL LRF YCV XVN DLP PVPQJ'F.

_____

—VXIYSPYV OYVXIXKDP

_____

HINTS (SEE PAGE 138): 16, 39

№13 THE VALUE IN KEEPING CITIZENS WELL-INFORMED

PCDGAVFPC FVP NPXNDP APCPJTDDS, TCL FSJTCCS

_____

TCL XNNJPIIGXCI XU EXLS TCL RGCL KGDD OTCGIV

_____

DGQP INGJGFI TF FVP LTKC XU LTS.

_____

—FVXRTI WPUUPJIXC

_____

HINTS (SEE PAGE 138): 10, 18

SUDOKU №8

8		9			2			
2	1	7						
				7				
	2		4	1				9
9		6		2		8		5
3				8	6		4	
				5				
						6	9	8
			3			4		7

SUDOKU №9

		4	3	6		1		9
							3	8
		5		8		4		
6				3	9			
	3						2	
			6	2				7
		6		9		2		
5	8							
9		2		7	6	5		

SUDOKU №10

	2			8				
		7				3		8
			6	4				1
	6		7			9		2
		8	9		4	1		
7		9			2		5	
8				7	6			
1		6				8		
				3			4	

SUDOKU №11

				5		9		
3			6					4
2	4	5			8			6
				6			1	3
4		7				2		9
6	3			2				
9			2			5	3	7
5					9			8
		4		3				

SUDOKU №12

	3	2		1	8			
			4		6	2		
	4			9			3	
		7						
3	2						5	9
						6		
	9			4			6	
		8	2		3			
			8	6		7	1	

SUDOKU №13

6				3			1	2
		2	9					8
					6		4	
		3	5	8				
4								7
				1	4	3		
	2		6					
1					5	2		
7	9			2				4

SUDOKU №14

						8		
8					7	2	6	
	9	6	8				4	
		4		7			9	
			5		8			
	1			6		4		
	4				6	9	1	
	7	2	1					5
		3						

SUDOKU №15

		1	6					
	7		8	5				
3		4			1			5
7				2		5		
8				1				2
	2		7					3
1			5			2		7
				2	6		3	
				9	1			

CALCUDOKU

CALCUDOKU №8

12×		1-		15×
2 :		9+	1-	
10×				1
	10+	1-		2 :
			3	

CALCUDOKU №9

1-		3+		3
12×		0-		7+
	6×		3-	
1-		7+		8+
	5			

CALCUDOKU №10

5	**8×**	**10+**		**1-**
3×		**2-**		
	6+			**1-**
6+		**5+**	**5**	
	3		**3-**	

CALCUDOKU №11

3	**2-**	**16+**		**3-**	**4-**
5 :		**8+**			
	120×			**3-**	**2 :**
			10×		
2	**3 :**			**10+**	
6	**20×**		**2-**		**2**

CALCUDOKU №12

2-	11+	5+		1-	
		3-		2	0-
15×		1-	4		
2 :			11+		11+
	1-				
10+		1-		2-	

CALCUDOKU №13

9+		5×		2	20×
16+			3	6 :	
3-		1-	1-		4+
	20×			1-	
7+			2		12×
	4+		1-		

FUTOSHIKI

FUTOSHIKI №8

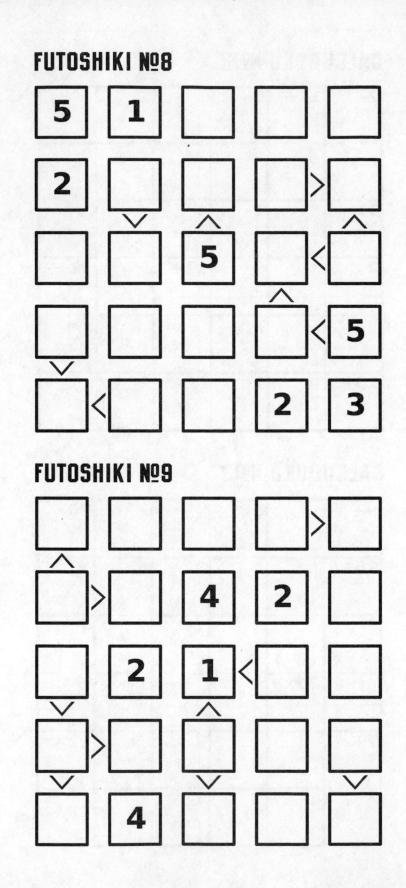

FUTOSHIKI №9

FUTOSHIKI №10

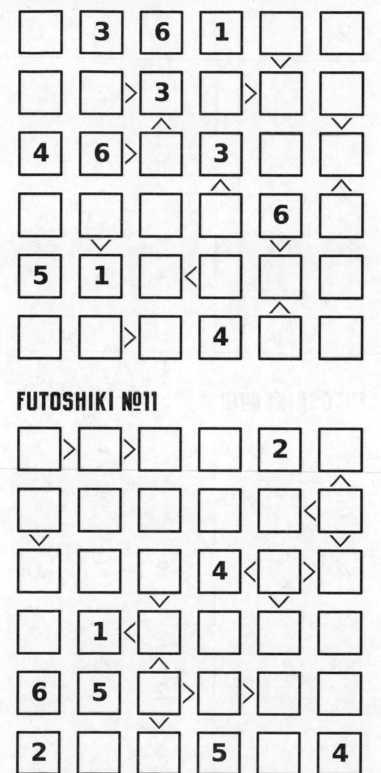

FUTOSHIKI №11

FUTOSHIKI №12

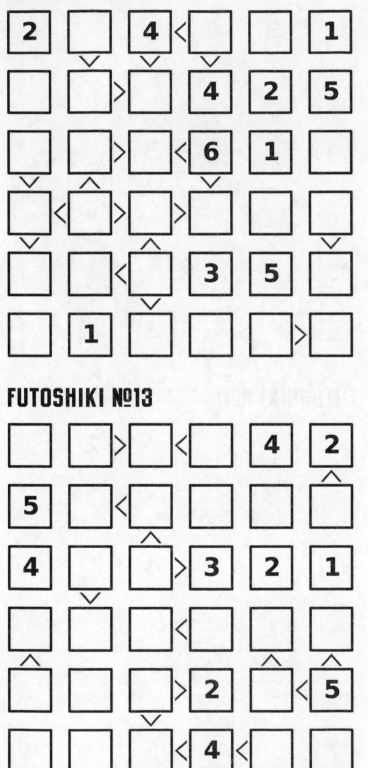

FUTOSHIKI №13

№7 TRICK OR TREAT

It's the day after Halloween, and four youngsters who are neighborhood pals are hanging out at Kyle's house and inventorying their remaining take from the previous night's trick-or-treating. There's also a lot of swapping going on, as everybody wants as much of their favorite type of candy they can trade for. Check out the clues below, and see whether you can figure out what costume each trick-or-treater donned last night, how many pieces of candy they now have in their inventories, and what type of candy is each one's favorite.

1. The trick-or-treat group includes Callie, the kid who dressed up as a cat last night, another who still has 40 treats to consume, and a fourth whose preferred treat is mini packets of candy bars.

2. Katie, who doesn't have 46 treats left in her bag this morning, has more than Kyle but less than Colin.

3. Neither Colin nor Kyle has a preference for soft fruit gummy candy or mini-bars.

4. Callie was not costumed as a clown or ghost last night, nor does she have 52 treats in her bag this morning.

5. Colin is not a big chocolates fan; Kyle did not wear a clown costume last night.

		Costume				No. of Treats				Fav Candy			
		cat	clown	doctor	ghost	40	45	46	52	chocolates	gummies	licorice	mini-bars
Child	Callie												
	Colin												
	Katie												
	Kyle												
Fav Candy	chocolates												
	gummies												
	licorice												
	mini-bars												
No. of Treats	40												
	45												
	46												
	52												

№8 A FRIENDLY/COMPETITIVE ROUND OF GOLF

Four guys who love to play golf and are pretty good at the game got together for a friendly but competitive round the other day. To amp up the competition, they got several bets going: big bets on low score and fewest putts; and much smaller individual hole-by-hole bets in a "skins game," in which every hole is contested separately and the winner of a hole gets paid a "skin" from each of the other players and also wins any carryover holes preceding it in which the best score was a tie. The clues below give fragmentary information as to who shot what in this round. See whether you can use the clues to piece together a full picture of who had the lowest score, who had the lowest number of putts, and how the skins game shook out.

1. The golfers include Greg, the golfer who shot the low round of 73, the golfer who took 35 putts during the round, and the one who won seven holes in the skins game.

2. A player whose score was three strokes lower than the next higher score had 34 putts in the round.

3. Jerry did not take 37 putts in the round, while another golfer who took 33 putts didn't record just one skins game win.

4. Gary's score for the round was higher than Jerry's but lower than Larry's.

5. The golfer with the best—that is, the lowest—score for the round did not have 37 putts, but Larry had 35 putts.

6. Gary did not shoot 78 for the round or take 37 putts. Larry didn't shoot 78 either, nor did he claim just one victorious hole in the skins game during the round.

7. Neither the golfer with 35 putts nor the one with 37 putts won six holes in the skins game.

		Total Score				No. of Putts				Skins game			
		73	76	78	81	33	34	35	37	1	4	6	7
Golfer	Greg												
	Gary												
	Larry												
	Jerry												
Skins game	1												
	4												
	6												
	7												
No. of Putts	33												
	34												
	35												
	37												

№ 9 GRADING PAPERS FOR COMPOSITION CLASS

It is the beginning of the fall semester at Middlestate College, and students in Professor Wright's freshman composition class have submitted their initial compositions—a 500-word essay on the topic of their choice. Wright has graded the papers, and the clues below provide information on the four that garnered the top grades in the class. This puzzle asks you to use the clues to link up each of the students who got the top grades with the topic they chose to write on, the grade they were given for their efforts, and the main criticism Professor Wright made regarding their essay. It could be a challenge, but you won't be graded on your answers.

1. Neither Daphne nor Lisa chose the status of off-campus housing as their essay topic.

2. Daphne received a higher grade than Lisa, but her grade was not as high as Bruce's.

3. Professor Wright did not criticize either Bruce or Chuck for a grammar mistake or for a couple misuses of vocabulary.

4. Daphne's grade was not A–, the topic of her essay was not modern art, and her writing was not criticized for vocabulary errors either.

5. Bruce didn't receive an A– grade either, and the topic of his essay was not the benefits of exercise or off-campus housing. The criticism Professor Wright leveled at him on his essay was not for flaws in its organization.

6. The essay criticized for its vocabulary lapses was not about the benefits of exercising, and the essay criticized for the excessive length of some of its sentences was not the one focused on modern art.

7. Chuck's grade was not A–.

| | | Grade | | | | Topic | | | | Criticism | | | |
		A+	A	A-	B+	modern art	exercise	football team	housing	grammar	sentence length	organization	vocabulary
Student	Bruce												
	Chuck												
	Daphne												
	Lisa												
Criticism	grammar												
	sentence length												
	organization												
	vocabulary												
Topic	modern art												
	exercise												
	football team												
	housing												

№10 FINDING A WEDDING VENUE

Cassie and Carl are ready to tie the knot, and Cassie (who wants her wedding to be in June) has been exploring options for the wedding, including the venue at which the wedding and reception will take place. She has come up with four venue options in workable locations and now is ready to decide which one to pick. The venue rental price, which just covers the cost of renting the space (food and drink, flowers, entertainment, and so on will be added later), is an important consideration, as well as any extra added feature each venue has that would make it a good choice. Luckily, each location Cassie zeroed in on still has a Saturday in June available (though the dates are all different), but she needs to move quickly to lock in a date. Using the clues below, see whether you can get a better sense of what venue rental choices Cassie has.

1. The historic mansion Cassie is considering isn't the venue that is offering a discount on rental of event furnishings, nor is it asking $3,200 in rent; the downtown hotel she has contacted is not the venue that has a large lawn available for outdoor activities, and its proposed rental fee is not $2,750.

2. The vineyard on the edge of town that hosts weddings is not available on June 10 but is available on a date later in June than the date the country club that Cassie is considering as the wedding site has available and is earlier than the date proposed by the hotel.

3. One of the venues that is proposing a rental fee $250 more than another venue has ample free parking available for wedding attendees.

4. The rental fees being asked by the hotel and vineyard are neither the highest nor lowest among the four venues.

5. The venue whose rental fee is $2,500 is not the one that has June 10 available. Nor does it have a large dance floor (the country club is the one that touts that feature).

6. The downtown hotel also is not available on June 10, nor does it offer free parking.

		Date Available				Feature				Rental charge			
		June 3	June 10	June 17	June 24	dance floor	free parking	large lawn	furn. discount	$2,500	$2,750	$3,000	$3,200
Venue Option	country club												
	downtown hotel												
	historic mansion												
	vineyard												
Rental charge	$2,500												
	$2,750												
	$3,000												
	$3,200												
Feature	dance floor												
	free parking												
	large lawn												
	furn. discount												

№11 FLIGHT ATTENDANTS

Four young flight attendants who became pals during their training classes have all been assigned to the same "hub" airport. They share an apartment near the airport, and early this morning, they left home for the airport together because they all are working morning flights to various locations. The clues below provide some fragmentary information on their work assignments today. See whether you can use the clues to get a full picture of what flights they will be staffing.

1. The group of four flight attendants consists of Pam, the person who is going to work flight 569, the guy whose flight leaves at 7:50 AM, and another whose flight is headed to Baltimore (BWI).

2. The flight that Paul is working takes off earlier than the one Patricia is working but later than Pete's flight.

3. The 7:25 AM flight that one of them is staffing is not going to Baltimore (BWI) or Charlotte (CLT).

4. Paul's flight is going to NYC LaGuardia (LGA); Pete's flight will not be landing at Baltimore (BWI).

5. Flight 3616 is not headed for Chicago O'Hare (ORD); and the flight to Charlotte (CLT) does not take off at 7:50 AM.

6. Flight 1386 does not take off 25 minutes after another flight that one of the four is on.

7. Patricia is not working flight 3616; Pete is working flight 569 (which is not slated to take off at 7:25 AM).

		Flight Number				Takeoff Time				Destination			
		569	1386	2574	3616	7:00 AM	7:25 AM	7:50 AM	8:10 AM	Baltimore (BWI)	Charlotte (CLT)	O'Hare (ORD)	LaGuardia (LGA)
Flt. Attendant	Pam												
	Patricia												
	Paul												
	Pete												
Destination	Baltimore (BWI)												
	Charlotte (CLT)												
	O'Hare (ORD)												
	LaGuardia (LGA)												
Takeoff Time	7:00 AM												
	7:25 AM												
	7:50 AM												
	8:10 AM												

№12 LAW FIRM ASSOCIATES

Four associates at a local law firm were gathered in the firm's lunchroom on a Friday afternoon having a casual get-together. One associate had just started work on Monday, and the other three were informally welcoming this newbie to the firm. People went around the table reviewing how long they had been with the firm, what partner they work most closely with, what type of law they were beginning to specialize in, and otherwise explaining what the new person might expect at the firm; all in all, it was a good bonding experience for the new associate. Take a look at the clues below, and see whether you can re-create some of the key elements of this "let's get acquainted" get-together.

1. The associates sitting around the lunch table included Adrienne, the new associate, the one who works closely with Ms. Peters, and the one developing expertise in tax law.

2. Neither woman at the table does work with Mr. Pierson.

3. Between Albert and the associate working in the firm's real estate section, one is the first-year associate and the other is the one that works a lot with Mr. Patterson.

4. The person who is developing a tax law practice is the one who has many assignments from Mr. Poston but is not a third-year associate.

5. Albert has been with the firm longer than Austin; Angela is not the one who works most closely with Ms. Peters.

6. Adrienne is not a fourth-year associate; and Austin's focus at the firm is not environmental law.

		Time at Firm				Partner				Law Specialty			
		just started	first year	third year	fourth year	Mr. Patterson	Ms. Peters	Mr. Pierson	Mr. Poston	business org.	envir. law	real estate	tax law
Associate	Adrienne												
	Albert												
	Angela												
	Austin												
Law Specialty	business org.												
	envir. law												
	real estate												
	tax law												
Partner	Mr. Patterson												
	Ms. Peters												
	Mr. Pierson												
	Mr. Poston												

CHAPTER 4
MORE-CHALLENGING PUZZLES

CROSSWORD

ACROSS

1. Wee
6. Scenery chewers
10. "Darn!"
14. Actress Shire of *Rocky*
15. Flair
16. Cork's country
17. Spanish fan
19. Brit's baby buggy
20. Taunt
21. _____-dieu (kneeling bench)
22. Hammer parts
23. Take exception to
25. Endings for "home," "bed," and "farm"
27. Parisian's "please"
30. Drive away
33. Type of school
34. Meadow
35. Build _____ egg (save)
36. Arikara
37. It might be blessed
39. European fish
40. Cake decorator
42. Takes a break
43. Body double, in Düsseldorf
47. Beer after a shot
48. Friendly, but dated, form of address to a man in England
52. Weather map area
53. Cousin of a bassoon
55. Competent
56. Nettle
57. Milanese's "Merry Christmas"
59. Law school newbie
60. "_____ girl!"
61. Passed fraudulently, as a check
62. Clutter
63. An "A" in NCAA: Abbr.
64. Words of agreement

DOWN

1. Legendary football coach Amos Alonzo _____
2. *The Godfather* group
3. Out of sorts?
4. Drivers' IDs
5. China's Chou En-____
6. English king who won at Agincourt
7. Central Asian mountain range
8. Double-checked
9. ____-Caps candy
10. Rescind
11. Large terriers
12. Lasting only for a short time
13. Sch. periods
18. Birthstone after sapphire
22. Bombarded, as with questions
24. Most muddy
26. *The Waste Land* monogram
28. Where to hear an aria
29. Body art, briefly
30. Police bust
31. Type of glands
32. Features of apartment doors
36. Replaces tiling mortar
38. Word for word
41. The Browns, on scoreboards
44. Judging groups
45. WSJ columnist Peggy
46. Narrow valley
49. Web money-back discount, slangily
50. _____ wrench
51. Requires
52. Gift tag word
54. Web crawlers, e.g.
57. Sheep's cry
58. Rap sheet letters

№15 FOREIGN-LANGUAGE TEST

1	2	3	4	5		6	7	8	9		10	11	12	13
14						15					16			
17					18						19			
20					21					22				
23				24			25	26						
			27			28							29	
30	31	32				33					34			
35					36				37	38				
39				40	41				42					
43			44				45	46						
	47						48				49	50	51	
52					53	54				55				
56				57				58						
59				60				61						
62				63				64						

1990S TRIVIA CHALLENGE

This world-renowned leader was elected president of his country in 1994, after having served 27 years in prison as a political prisoner. Who is this person?

This English pop group formed in 1994, and their first single, "Wannabe," became a worldwide hit. What is the name of the group?

ACROSS

1. Revise, as legislation
6. Young cow
10. Biblical beast of burden
13. Film
14. Person drawing a bead
15. Cable channel
16. Classroom contest
18. Eastern "way"
19. Expunge
20. Internet message
22. Unruffled
26. Grid of fine lines on an eyepiece
28. Come in second in a horse race
29. Irascible
31. Songbird
32. Canyon feature
33. Awards show hosts
36. Downed
37. Day play
39. Modern cinematic visual effects, briefly
40. Certain EVs
42. What 40 Acrosses don't need
43. _____ of Sandwich
44. Stadium ticket info
46. Bowling alley button
47. "Earth," for "heart"
49. Manuscript marks
50. Corkwood
51. Put forward
54. Fancy neckwear
55. Summit . . . as represented by the shape of the groups of circled squares and the words inside those squares
61. Docs' org.
62. Colorado park
63. Declaim
64. ___ card (phone insert)
65. Suffix with "gag" or "joke"
66. Seasonal visitor

DOWN

1. Mornings, for short
2. Item in a bucket
3. Genesis name
4. Common soccer score
5. Expunge
6. Smokes, briefly
7. Yellow hues
8. General in gray
9. Leisure hours
10. Executive's accessory
11. Symbol of slowness
12. Winter wrap
14. ___ Gasteyer
17. EU memb.
21. Catchall abbreviation
22. Water balloon impact sound
23. Overjoy
24. Tanzanian metropolis
25. Cry from Bill the Cat
27. Fencing equipment
29. Intelligent humor
30. Pedro's pal
32. Haile Selassie disciple
34. Everglades bird
35. Delta deposits
37. Knotted cord craftworks
38. Indian bread
41. Lower limbs
43. Doer's suffix
45. Ascribe
46. Numerical relationships
47. Arafat's successor
48. Tennis star _____ Osaka
49. Spy org.
52. Nonpareil
53. John, Paul and George: Abbr.
56. Düsseldorf direction
57. Gun group initials
58. Go for the bronze?
59. Polo Grounds legend
60. Princess tormentor

№16 ON THE HEIGHTS

1	2	3	4	5			6	7	8	9		10	11	12
13						14						15		
16					17							18		
				19						20	21			
22	23	24	25				26	27					
28						29	30						
31					32			33				34	35
36				37			38			39			
40			41			42				43			
		44			45				46				
47	48							49					
50					51	52	53						
54				55	56					57	58	59	60
61				62				63				
64				65				66				

THINK ABOUT IT

The more physically active one's lifestyle is, the better one will do in retaining cognitive functions as one ages. Aerobic exercise training, in particular, has been shown to help in improving cognitive functions even in adults as young as 20, although the effect is greater as one gets older.

ACROSS

1. Droop
4. Restaurant or computer offering
8. Made crow sounds
13. "Put ___ Happy Face"
14. Neighbor of Nigeria
15. Tribe of Israel
16. Criticizes harshly
18. Dilutes
19. Harry's VP
20. Lacks the wherewithall to
22. Agitate
23. Tower of London guards
27. Contraption
29. Sixth sense, for short
30. Hugs, symbolically
31. Madison Square Garden, e.g.
33. Old Testament song
35. Soviet flag symbols
40. Licorice-like flavoring
41. Herman's Hermits lead Peter
42. GOP org.
43. Major TV network
46. Sty
49. Pol's self-serving appropriation
52. Genealogical diagram
54. Infant's garment
55. Made a mistake
56. Storybook elephant
58. Nitwits . . . or a way to describe the starts of 16-, 23-, 35-, and 49-Across
61. Christopher of *Superman*
62. _____ Island (New York Harbor landmark)
63. New York Mets div.
64. Thing of value
65. "No returns"
66. Dover's state: Abbr.

DOWN

1. Kind of energy
2. Like a clock with hands
3. The _____ (country surrounded by Senegal)
4. My, in Versailles
5. Suffix with differ or persist
6. Bridget Fonda, to Jane
7. Risky
8. Having a short snooze
9. "_____ in the dark"
10. Hardwood used in aging bourbon
11. Hallow finish
12. AMA membs.
14. Prohibit
17. Old word meaning "old hags"
21. 45-degree compass pts.
23. Brewski
24. Peak near Taormina
25. Breadbasket item
26. Several
28. Nickname for a Special Forces soldier
32. Cape ___, MA
34. King's ceremonial staff, to a Brit
35. Stringed instrument
36. The "A" in AD
37. Germs
38. Inside info
39. Potting need
44. ___-relief
45. Yalta's peninsula
47. Gofer's job
48. Sewing implement
50. Scoundrel
51. Staggers
53. '50s Ford flop
55. Interjections occasionally heard in Canada
56. Bikini top
57. Monogram of the Dem. candidate for pres. in 1952 and 1956
59. *Aladdin* prince
60. "___ the season . . ."

№17 A LITTLE WORDPLAY

1	2	3	■	■	4	5	6	7	■	8	9	10	11	12
13			■	14					■	15				
16			17						■	18				

DID YOU KNOW?

People in Europe used the Roman numeral system until the 13th century, when it gradually was replaced by the much more user-friendly Hindu–Arabic numbering system we use today.

ACROSS

1. Ireland, poetically
5. Wild hog
9. "What ___ mind reader?"
13. Capture
14. Wight and Man
16. Country music partner of Brooks
17. *Caddyshack* actor
19. Edison's middle name
20. Canon camera model
21. Robin Williams TV role
23. Up to, briefly
24. Manicurist's board
27. *Gunsmoke* setting
29. Badger
30. Sculler's need
32. Upper-crust types
33. Unexciting, plain
35. Civil rights activist Parks
38. German town
39. Classic construction toy set
42. African horned beast, for short
44. McDonald's arches, e.g.
45. "Fine by me"
48. Lotus-_____ (figures in the *Odyssey*)
50. Furrow
52. Clean Air Act org.
53. Currency not backed by gold or some other valuable commodity
56. Church leader
58. "To ___ is human, . .   ."
59. God of love
60. Salary
61. Make revisions to
63. Alternatives to hot pants
68. Actress Cannon
69. Novelist Jong
70. Ark builder
71. Dispatched
72. Gets the picture
73. Kind of pool or therapy

DOWN

1. And so on: Abbr.
2. "Go team!"
3. 1950s White House nickname
4. "When pigs fly!"
5. Popular pens
6. ___ Kosh B'Gosh clothing
7. San Antonio landmark
8. Lay down new grass
9. Toothpaste tube letters
10. Worked on more than one thing at the same time
11. Requested politely
12. Wall Street professional
15. Worsted suit cloth
18. Toy that does tricks
22. Horse of the Year, 1960-64
24. Expire
25. Impair the appearance of
26. Related to the principle that all people should have the same rights and opportunities
27. Slobber
28. Gasoline brand
31. Parenthesis, essentially
34. IQ test pioneer
36. ___-mo replay
37. Steamed
40. _____ *Rae* (Sally Field film)
41. Singer Rawls
42. Inserts more paper into (a copier)
43. Changer of locks?
46. Gibbon, for one
47. Pirate's cry
49. River of northern Europe
51. Heavy, durable furniture wood
54. Gritty crime films, briefly
55. *Sesame Street* Muppet
57. Telling fibs
60. Educ. TV or radio spots
62. Demolition letters
64. "Rocks"
65. Fish eggs
66. Whup
67. Any ship

№18 AUTO SHOW

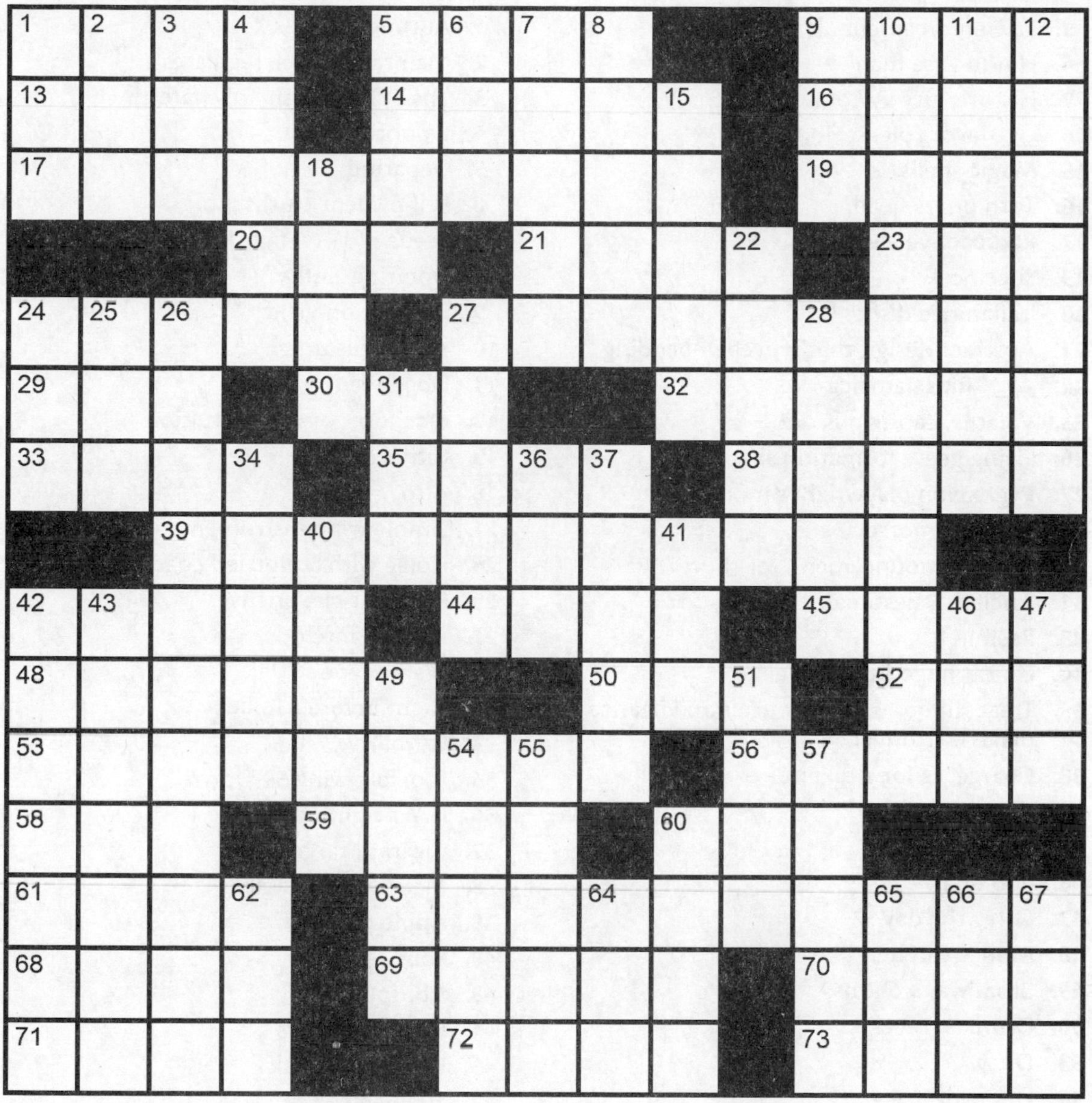

THINK ABOUT IT

Pattern recognition is an important cognitive capacity that enables a person to match information received with information retrieved from memory. It is a key aspect of inductive logic, which is the basis for all scientific inquiry. One's pattern recognition skills can be improved with practice.

ACROSS

1. Law enforcement alert initials
4. Hindu wise man
9. Historic city SW of Rome
14. ____ favor (please, in Spanish)
15. Magic spells
16. Turn on its head
17. Radioactive element
19. Succinct
20. Italian rice dishes
21. Abstract design that is eyeball-bending
22. _____ Rios, Jamaica
23. Volatile, capricious
26. Flying geese formation shape
27. *Pygmalion* playwright's monogram
29. Feedbag morsel
30. Pilot's announcement, for short
31. Ancient Palestinian ascetic
33. Besmirch
34. Guitar fingerboard ridge
35. Treat rubber with chemicals and heat to make it stronger
38. Charge, as for a taxi ride
41. Chunk
42. Itty-bitty bite
46. Pub quaff
47. Carry the day
48. Mouse catcher
49. Broadway's *6 Rms___ Vu*
50. Drunken revel
53. Ditty
54. Honeydew, e.g.
55. More succinct
58. Runway walker
59. Marked by regal beauty
60. Most suitable
61. "_____ live nephew of my Uncle Sam . . . "
62. Package delivery co.
63. Piquant
64. Kind of spray
65. Ballpark fig.

DOWN

1. Authorize
2. Maintains order, regulates
3. The Fuller salesman's wares
4. Opportunity
5. Departed
6. Self-evident truths
7. Scene of WWI fighting
8. Doctrine: Suffix
9. Production yield
10. Asparagus unit
11. Dog breed
12. One form of college tuition
13. Citrus drink
18. Also
21. Simple wind instrument
24. Horse with a mottled coat
25. Back muscle, briefly
27. African antelope
28. Waffle type
32. Night before a holiday
33. Bar bill
34. Mo. following 59-Down
36. N.Y. neighbor
37. Clearasil target
38. Marvelous, slangily
39. Apple pie order
40. Ebbs
43. Abrupt, vocally
44. Baseball rosters
45. Himalayan peak
47. 100 percent
48. Duplicates
51. Traction aid
52. Honda's luxury brand
53. "My country" follower
56. Hurricane tracking agcy.
57. Prison room
58. *Les* ____ (Broadway hit musical, for short)
59. Winter mo.

№19 BORRROWINGS FROM THE ROMAN PANTHEON

1	2	3	■	4	5	6	7	8	■	9	10	11	12	13
14			■	15					■	16				
17			18						■	19				
20								■	21					■
22			■			23		24					■	25
26			■	27	28		■	29			■	30		
31			32			■	33			■	34			
■		35			36				37			■		
38	39	40		■	41			■	42			43	44	45
46			■	47			■	48			■	49		
50			51			52		■			53			
■	54					■	55		56	57				
58					■	59								
60				■	61					■	62			
63				■	64				■	65				

2000S TRIVIA CHALLENGE

Name the animated film released in 2001 that tells the story of a fairy-tale ogre who falls in love.

Who became chancellor of Germany in 2005 and held that post until 2021?

ACROSS

1. Like Montezuma
8. Learned person
15. Glacial debris pile
16. Bull-like
17. Inactivity
18. Claims, as in a court case
19. One with a lot to offer?
21. Container weight
22. Corral
23. Song and dance, e.g.
24. Does without
26. Football video game name
28. Radiator sound
29. When it's broken, that's good
30. Many of the Marshall Islands
34. Took a course?
35. Ceramic artisans
37. Painter's medium
38. Complicated situations
40. Miss after marriage
41. Paleontologist's discovery
42. Spiel
44. Used the oven
45. ___ spell (took a load off)
48. Chinese dynasty
49. Absorbs, with "up"
50. Putting off until later what should be done now
55. Most ventilated
56. Afternoon performance
57. Pinkish
58. Yukon Mountie of old TV
59. Raged
60. Service deliveries

DOWN

1. Gulf VIP: Var.
2. Certain basketball defense
3. Dissertations
4. Winter cap parts
5. Bibliography assemblers
6. Biscotti flavoring
7. Straight, at the bar
8. Said
9. Their days are numbered
10. Waikiki wiggle
11. Pizza herb
12. Hybrid feline offspring
13. Regarding
14. Takes ten
20. Flat
24. Bogus
25. Toy with a tail
26. "Welcome" site
27. Aliens, for short
29. ASAP
31. Investigates
32. Queue
33. Winter coaster
35. Vegetable that rolls
36. Goof up
39. More out to lunch
41. Christian rite
43. Sampled
44. Straw hat
45. Sail supports
46. Running wild
47. Trunk
49. Entrap
51. 500 sheets
52. Little devils
53. Brightly colored
54. Grant and Lee: Abbr.

№20 NO THEME, BUT CHALLENGING

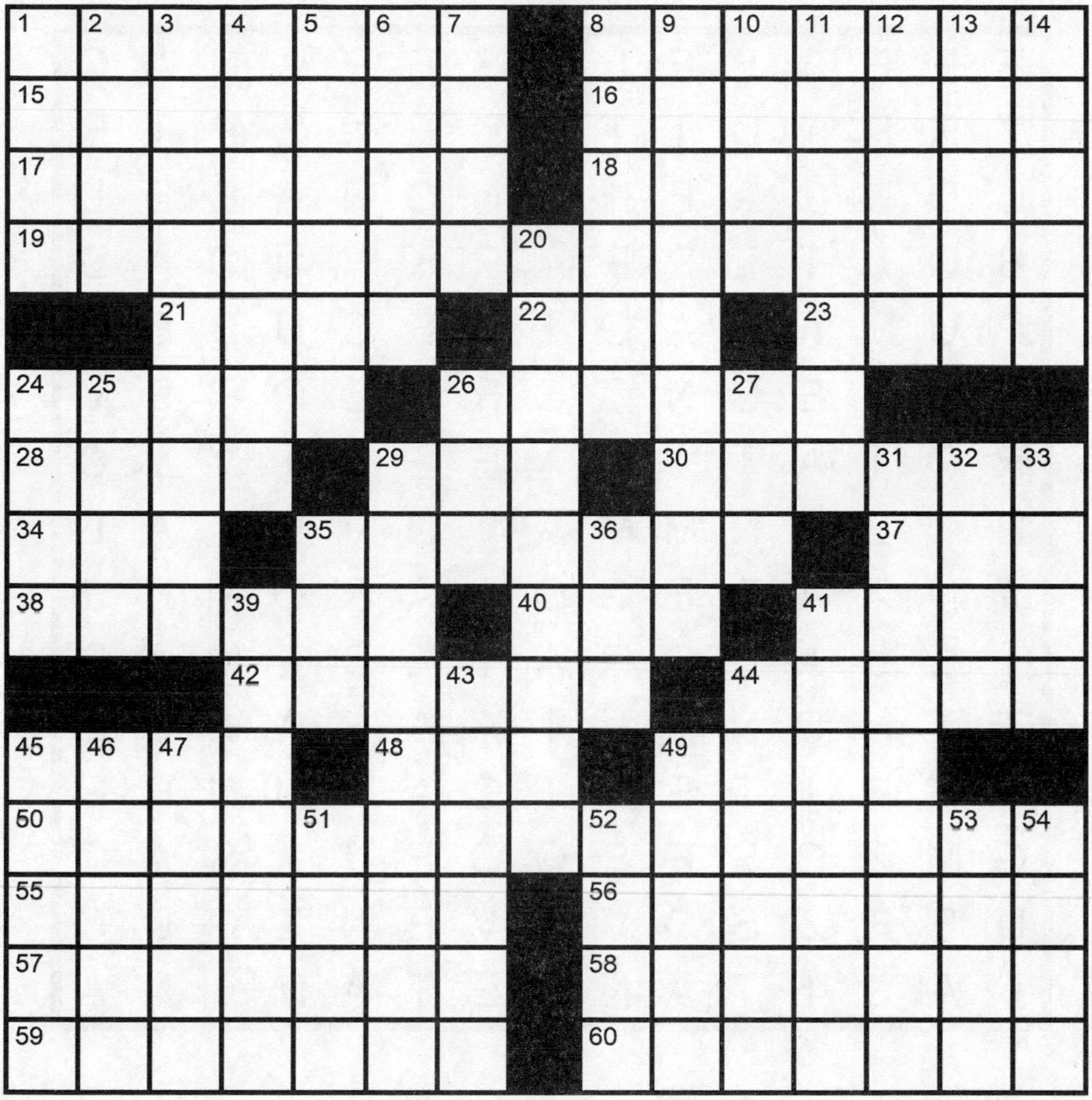

THINK ABOUT IT

While it is clear that our cognitive abilities change as we and our brains age, cognitive decline is not inevitable. Every individual has different results, and some of the possible factors for the variation in results are things we can exert some control over—our overall health, our lifestyle, and our level of brain activity.

№14 ALTERNATING VOWELS AND CONSONANTS

```
E E E C L E L Z S E P A N A C
Y R R T D T T H D E N E P I R
C D U O A E N A N O N A B E L
B O L T L R P A R K N U O A D
P U M A A A O I C E C U B E R
K O T E C N G C R I B O R E M
R O T A T I G A E E R I V Y C
E O B A N M M A V D V E L A L
V N T A T E G O I A R O M E J
I E L A B O R A T E D E M A D
T T N O N A H I A A R A W E G
I I K I T E V T C A N U N R R
G M Z O S E S O O E J A S A O
U E R Z S O V A V E N E G D C
F A J I T A N D E T A M I N A
```

AGITATOR	CANAPES	FUGITIVE	ORIGINAL
AGONIZE	COMET	GALORE	POTATO
AMERICAN	CUBIC	GENEVA	REMOVE
ANATOMICAL	DECORATE	ICE CUBE	REVERE
ANIMATED	DELIBERATE	LABOR	RIPENED
ARENA	DERIVATIVES	LEBANON	SENATOR
AVOCADO	ELABORATE	MINARET	VENISON
BUTANE	ENAMEL	NATURE	
CAMERA	EVOCATIVE	ONE-TIME	
CANADA	FAJITA	ORATOR	

№15 GREEK ISLANDS

```
L E R O S S O G R O M A I I X
I N I R O T N A S O N I T S P
I M G R R S N K K Y T H N O S
Q X Y Q Y A O Y S M A E P S A
Y K A S S P T R Y C S C V O R
S B A P E H C K A O X A V I A
O S H L I E O R N P I R Y H A
H E O R Y N J F S N I H N Y Z
T S A R O M I L O S S T N D E
N T K S D S N L M O T O N R T
Y E X O B N A O A H S M I A E
K P M D S H A B S T P A S H R
A S T Y P A L A I A H S O D C
Z O S E D O H R T P A A B E O
M R C O R F U M O R Z R S L Y
N A X O S C O V A A N G E O Y
R P Z T V S A D A K F E L S S
```

AMORGOS	IOS	MYKONOS	SKOPELOS
ANDROS	ITHACA	NAXOS	SKYROS
ANTIPAROS	KALYMNOS	PAROS	SPETSES
ASTYPALAIA	KARPATHOS	PATMOS	SYMI
CEPHALONIA	KOS	PAXI	SYROS
CHIOS	KYTHIRA	PSARA	THASOS
CORFU	KYTHNOS	RHODES	TINOS
CRETE	LEFKADA	SAMOS	ZAKYNTHOS
DELOS	LEROS	SAMOTHRACE	
EVIA	LESBOS	SANTORINI	
HYDRA	MILOS	SIFNOS	

№16 RIVERS OF THE WORLD

```
G B V R N O D T A N M S N I S H D
Q A U O I Q K A X I O R A N E L N
E M N T L R H N R Z B E A D M W Y
A Z I G E G A A A E M M P U A D P
N T T S E T A R H P U E U S H O R
N O I G S S B A E D C E K L T C C
U Y Z G N I O P A O S D W O O K H
U A E A R A S R S E Q N M L N C O
T R B E M I Y S C X T A O Y F G S
D R M I P A S N I R C R I H N N N
N U A I N E E J X P A G L O A B A
E M Z E S R B H L D P O C K H Y D
I N L E W S U U O Y E I E X F I R
P B I A N D O C N N O R I N O C O
E L L E S O M U I A I O D E R M J
R T P O S P H H R O D D N O K U Y
S E N F N M R R L I W O L L E Y E
```

AMAZON	EUPHRATES	MURRAY	SEINE
AMU DARYA	GANGES	NILE	SNAKE
AMUR	HUDSON	ODER	ST. LAWRENCE
BRAZOS	INDUS	OHIO	THAMES
COLORADO	JORDAN	ORINOCO	TIGRIS
COLUMBIA	LENA	PARANA	VOLGA
CONGO	LOIRE	PECOS	YANGTZE
DANUBE	MEKONG	POTOMAC	YELLOW
DNEIPER	MISSISSIPPI	RHINE	YUKON
DON	MISSOURI	RHONE	ZAMBEZI
ELBE	MOSELLE	RIO GRANDE	

№17 CELESTIAL CONSTELLATIONS

```
X S U N I H P L E D C B R R S
S U R U A T L I B R A P O E A
I U R P N O I R O P S G N T N
L A E C E T U S A E S C I I T
A S P H O R O L O G I U M C L
E P A U P E S B R A O R S U I
R I A G S E G E D S P S I L A
O S Z N I E C E U U E A N U R
B C U R M T M Z R S I M A M D
A E A I B O T O M P A I C O Y
N S N P R O J A M S I N A C H
O I B D R A X S R C A O Z A I
R Q N D M I U N A I A R N R D
O A K A N I C Q Y H U N Y D D
C B S E P R U O A L J S C L T
A R O R A I S U R U A T N E C
U H O T L S C Y G N U S L Q R
P C E A Y W K S E L U C R E H
S R O G R I V L U P U S P U O
```

ANDROMEDA	CENTAURUS	HERCULES	PHOENIX
ANTLIA	CEPHEUS	HOROLOGIUM	PISCES
APUS	CETUS	HYDRA	RETICULUM
AQUARIUS	CORONA	LEO	SAGITTARIUS
AQUILA	BOREALIS	LIBRA	SCORPIUS
ARIES	CRATER	LUPUS	TAURUS
CANCER	CRUX	LYNX	URSA MAJOR
CANIS MAJOR	CYGNUS	LYRA	URSA MINOR
CANIS MINOR	DELPHINUS	ORION	VIRGO
CAPRICORNUS	DRACO	PEGASUS	
CASSIOPEIA	GEMINI	PERSEUS	

```
U K U K O E K A E K K W H T W
S O R P R Z V K R D K O P E K
E T B E W A O A U I Y K O O K
K K S O J R K C A S P A N K L
A I H Y T E E A M K S R H K O
Y T D S N Z E R T K F K C K F
A R Y S I T K N U O Z A I D N
K E D S K K A L K Q A N K E I
K C K P B I K N U C K L E K K
K K A N D I N S K Y A I U K I
N I X N N O A H G R O K K E D
H K T G K K K D E K L O C R K
A N L K A K E X K K K L O T I
K O O P A K C I K C O K N S D
I M O H K T R I H O D A K S K
A K N A C K I U N L I T R Z C
L I Y E S E K N E K A A K A A
B C D O P K A K I C K B A C K
U K I I E D H K N U K S Z Y C
K K G R E K K M O M O K O K A
```

ACK-ACK	KEOKUK	KISHKE	KOOKY
CHUKKER	KEYSTROKE	KIT KAT	KOPEK
DIK-DIK	KHAKI	KNACK	KRAKATOA
GROKKED	KICK	KNAPSACK	KRAKEN
KAFKA	KICKAPOO	KNEE-JERK	KRAKOW
KANDINSKY	KICKBACK	KNICKKNACK	KUBLAI KHAN
KANKAKEE	KIDSKIN	KNOCK	SKULKING
KAPOK	KINFOLK	KNUCKLE	SKUNK
KARAOKE	KINKY	KODIAK	TIKTOK
KAYAK	KIOSK	KOKOMO	TREKKED
KEN KESEY	KIRK	KOLKATA	YAKKED

№19 MISSING VOWELS

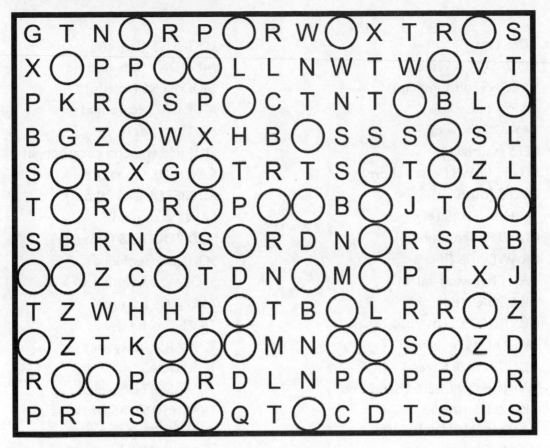

The puzzle grid contains no vowels, only circles where the vowels should be. Your challenge is to fill in the vowels as you locate the key words. Every circle will be filled when the puzzle is completely solved.

ADDRESS	DEPTH	ORCHID	SPORTS
ALOUD	ETHOS	PROTEST	SPRINT
APPEAL	EXTRAS	QUEST	TEETH
BALLOTS	GARAGE	REAPER	TELL
BARN	JAMB	REBOOT	TRAIN
BEEPER	JOSTLE	REPRINT	TROPE
BOOST	METEOR	RESPECT	TWIST
BUZZER	NATURE	SORTED	UPPER
CHURN	NODULE	SPLINT	

№20 SOME MINOR LEAGUE BASEBALL TEAM NAMES

ACES (reno)

AQUASOX (everett)

BARONS (birmingham)

BATS (louisville)

BAYSOX (bowie)

BEES (salt lake)

BLUE CLAWS (jersey shore)

BULLS (durham)

CHIHUAHUAS (el paso)

CLIPPERS (columbus)

CRAWDADS (hickory)

DASH (winston-salem)

DRAGONS (dayton)

DUST DEVILS (tri-city)

EMERALDS (eugene)

FIGHTIN PHILS (reading)

FLYING SQUIRRELS (richmond)

GRIZZLIES (fresno)

HAMMERHEADS (jupiter)

HOPS (hillsboro)

IRONBIRDS (aberdeen)

ISOTOPES (albuquerque)

LOONS (great lakes)

LUGNUTS (lansing)

MISSIONS (san antonio)

MUD HENS (toledo)

MUDCATS (carolina)

NUTS (modesto)

QUAKES (rancho cucamonga)

RAWHIDE (visalia)

RUBBERDUCKS (akron)

SAINTS (st. paul)

SOD POODLES (amarillo)

SOUNDS (nashville)

STORM (lake elsinore)

TARPONS (tampa)

TIDES (norfolk)

TINCAPS (ft. wayne)

TORTUGAS (daytona)

TOURISTS (asheville)

TRASH PANDAS (rocket city)

TRAVELERS (arkansas)

WIND SURGE (wichita)

YARD GOATS (hartford)

```
S T O R M Z S S D A D W A R C
H N R T X U M L S N O O L S F
O S O A R R D N L N N S T I X
P R I I S A E C A U A A G E E
S E U X S H V P A U B H S G S
Z T F B D S P E H T T S R L W
S E N U B E I A L I S U E T A
L E M I R E U M N E S R P O L
I K P S A H R P L D R Y P U C
V S T O I S H D N I A S I R E
E D D H T I O I U Y B S L I U
D N C U L O W Q A C D E C S L
T U N S P B S R U A K G E T B
S O J D A G D I E A R S A S L
U S O Y N G B H T I K R C E U
D S S I O A R I Z X P E D D G
D O Y A R E N Z O O V R S I N
X L T O M C L S N D A S H T U
F S N M A I A S A G U T R O T
N S A P E U I R O N B I R D S
C H S S Q T R N E D I H W A R
H C Y A C E S D L A R E M E X
```

CRYPTOGRAM

№14 CHEERLEADING CAN LOSE ITS LUSTER

NHGOCJEO N WUFHHAJH AHNGGTITI FW N ZCWG

_____

XTHFEOGAJH VCZKNSFCS FA LCJ ONPT OFZ NHH GC

_____

LCJIWTHA, OFW GNWGT MTVCZTW PTIL XCJMGAJH

_____

QOTS OT GNUTW GC VCZKHFZTSGFSE CGOTI KTCKHT.

_____

—VONIHTW XFVUTSW

_____

HINT (SEE PAGE 138): 19

№15 CHECKING OUT UNFAMILIAR TERRITORY

RX PBNQQ CSF ZXNPX LISE XGJQSINFASC, NCU FBX

_____

XCU SL NQQ STI XGJQSIACO RAQQ KX FS NIIAMX

_____

RBXIX RX PFNIFXU NCU VCSR FBX JQNZX LSI FBX

_____

LAIPF FAEX.

_____

—F. P. XQASF

_____

HINT (SEE PAGE 138): 8

№16 USE YOUR FREE TIME THOUGHTFULLY

NSVEU GKWW BCSE FDVEK OCOKIQF. QPKB VEK WMXK

_____

SIASQ UMVOCIUF. UMFAVEU QPKO VIU QPKME JVWSK

_____

GMWW IKJKE HK XICGI. MODECJK QPKO VIU QPKB

_____

GMWW HKACOK QPK HEMNPQKFQ NKOF MI V SFKLSW

_____

WMLK.

_____

—EVWDP GVWUC KOKEFCI

_____

HINT (SEE PAGE 138): 11

№17 PERSEVERANCE UNDER PRESSURE PAYS

PRLS EBJ XLF DSFB V FDXRF KTVIL VSU LCLGEFRDSX

_____

XBLA VXVDSAF EBJ, FDTT DF ALLYA VA FRBJXR EBJ

_____

IBJTU SBF RVSX BS V YDSJFL TBSXLG, SLCLG XDCL JK

_____

FRLS, QBG FRVF DA OJAF FRL KTVIL VSU FDYL FRVF

_____

FRL FDUL PDTT FJGS.

_____

—RVGGDLF MLLIRLG AFBPL

_____

HINT (SEE PAGE 138): 15

№18 PRACTICE MAKES PERFECT

VRKVFFVSKV YJ PS PIU CLS NE UIPYSYSX PST

_____

OPNYUHPUYLS. CV TL SLU PKU IYXOUFE NVKPHJV CV

_____

OPZV ZYIUHV LI VRKVFFVSKV, NHU IPUOVI CV OPZV

_____

UOLJV NVKPHJV CV OPZV PKUVT IYXOUFE. CV PIV COPU

_____

CV IVBVPUVTFE TL. VRKVFFVSKV, UOVS, YJ SLU PS PKU

_____

NHU P OPNYU.

_____

—PIYJULUFV

_____

HINT (SEE PAGE 138): 29

№19 MAKING DONALD COME ALIVE

CRVSCFVXR VE QVPPBHBRF... VFE ICROYCOB VE FUB

_____

ICROYCOB XP TCHVTCFYHB. XYH SXEF QVPPVTYIF NXW

_____

KCE FX QBABIXJ FUB TCHFXXR'E YRRCFYHCI WYF

_____

EBBSVROIL RCFYHCI CRCFXSL PXH UYSCRE CRQ

_____

CRVSCIE.

_____

—KCIF QVERBL

_____

HINTS (SEE PAGE 138): 3, 14

SUDOKU №16

				5	8	3	7	
	5	3						8
8				6		5	9	
			1	7		2		
			5		4			
		7		9	2			
	3	9		2				5
7						9	6	
	4	5	9	1				

SUDOKU №17

		3		2				
	5		7				6	9
4	9				5			
2		5						
7		1				6		4
						5		3
			1				5	6
9	7				4		8	
				6		7		

SUDOKU №18

				7		6		3
	6	1			3	9		
	2						4	
	9	7			5			
				4				
			2			5	9	
	7						3	
		8	4			7	1	
6		5		3				

SUDOKU №19

	6		8			1		
				2				
		1			3	6	7	
		6	2			9	8	
2								6
	3	9			1	2		
	8	7	9			3		
				7				
		5			4		9	

SUDOKU №20

					8			
	5		7			3		2
				9			1	4
7		3	5					
1			6		2			3
					7	4		5
8	2			5				
9		1			3		6	
			8					

SUDOKU №21

	2	3		9	4			
			3				5	
9				6		1		
		8		5	6		9	
	4		8	3		7		
		4		2				5
	7				3			
			7	8		3	1	

CALCUDOKU №14

2-		1-	2-		8+
1-				4-	
4+		1-			0-
9+			1-		
24×		12×		1-	
	2		3		5

CALCUDOKU №15

5+	12×	6 :		1-	
		5 :	90×	7+	
4-	9+				1-
			0-		
120×		36×		9+	
					5

CALCUDOKU №16

1-	3 :		2 :		30×
	6×			4-	
30×		72×	5		2-
	4-			6×	
2 :		90×	4		2-
	4				

CALCUDOKU №17

13+		11+		12×	10+
			4×		
3 :		6+		30×	
48×			30×		2×
3-		7+		30×	
	1		2		

CALCUDOKU №18

15+		5×		6 :	2-
		72×			
10×			144×		1
4×	12×	15×	3+		
				0-	1-
11+					

CALCUDOKU №19

6	1-		1-		18×
16+		6+		2×	
		6	3		1-
3×	4-		3-	2-	
	12+				12+
2 :			6		

FUTOSHIKI

FUTOSHIKI №14

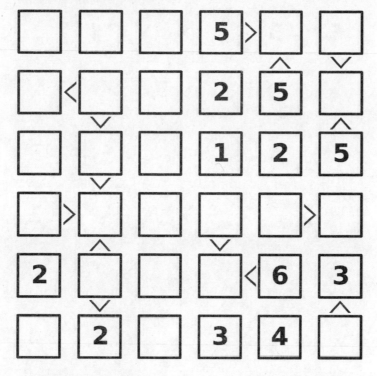

FUTOSHIKI №15

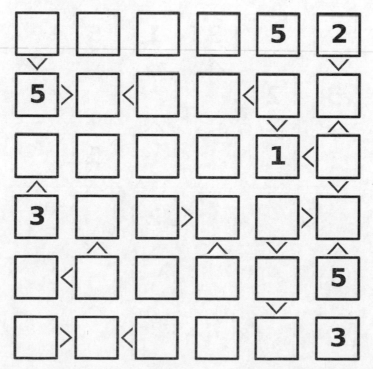

MORE-CHALLENGING PUZZLES   121

FUTOSHIKI №16

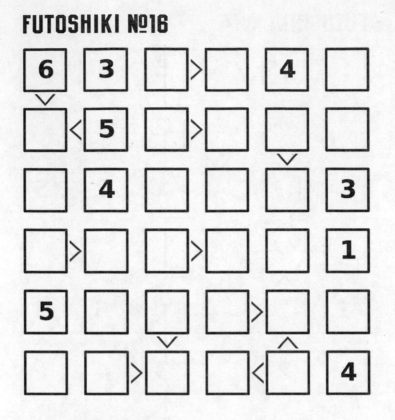

FUTOSHIKI №17

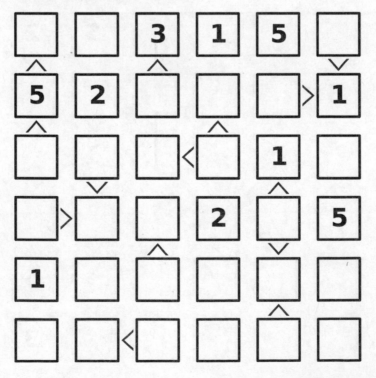

FUTOSHIKI №18

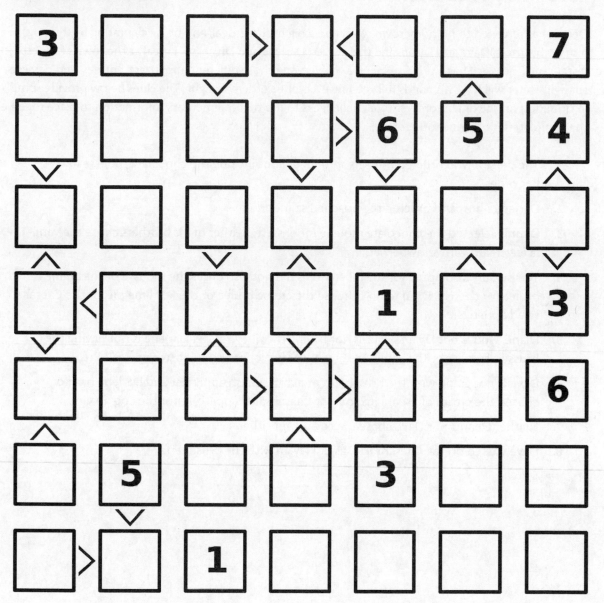

DID YOU KNOW?

The oldest known puzzle is a dissection-of-a-square puzzle described by Archimedes around 250 BCE. Similar to a tangram, the Archimedes puzzle consists of 14 irregularly shaped polygons that can be assembled to form a perfect square.

№13 PRIX FIXE DINING

Dennis has returned to his hometown to finalize a big business deal, and he is celebrating by treating his two brothers, Dave and Dylan, and their wives, Darlene and Diane, to a meal at the town's fanciest restaurant. The place has a prix fixe menu and everyone chose different appetizers, entrees, and desserts, so their waiter will have his hands full keeping everyone's orders straight. The clues below provide some information on the diners' orders. Your challenge is to use that fragmentary information to piece together the complete set of dinner orders.

1. The person who ordered brussels sprouts did not include the chocolate mousse in her order.

2. Darlene's husband ordered the poached salmon.

3. Dennis selected the chocolate mousse for dessert; neither of his brothers chose the vanilla ice cream with strawberries.

4. The person who opted for the lobster tails did not also order the mousse or the crème brulee for dessert. Dylan didn't choose the crème brulee or the key lime pie, or the Caesar salad appetizer.

5. Diane, who is not Dylan's wife, is not having the ribeye steak. Darlene is not having the brussels sprouts or the vanilla ice cream confection, nor the lobster or steak.

6. Dave is not going with the bruschetta or acorn squash appetizer and Darlene has not chosen the cream of asparagus soup or Caesar salad appetizer nor the coq au vin.

7. Neither Dennis nor Dave chose the coq au vin either.

8. Dave passed on the Caesar salad, as did Dylan with the bruschetta.

		Appetizer					Entrée					Dessert				
		acorn squash	asparagus soup	bruschetta	brussels sprouts	Caesar salad	coq au vin	eggplant	lobster tails	salmon	ribeye steak	choc. mousse	crème brulee	key lime pie	red velvet cake	ice cream
Diner	Darlene															
	Dave															
	Dennis															
	Diane															
	Dylan															
Dessert	choc. mousse															
	crème brulee															
	key lime pie															
	red velvet cake															
	ice cream															
Entrée	coq au vin															
	eggplant															
	lobster tails															
	salmon															
	ribeye steak															

DID YOU KNOW?

While Sudoku uses numbers, it is not a math game but a logic game. Still, much math has been used to thoroughly analyze the game. Among the conclusions reached through math calculations is that the minimum number of seeded numbers/clues needed to ensure that the typical 9x9 Sudoku has only one possible solution is 17 (18 for grids using 180-degree rotational symmetry, as do the ones in this book). Any fewer seeded numbers/clues than these, and there might be two or more possible solutions possible, which is a no-no for any puzzle.

№ 14 SPRINGTIME LANDSCAPING

Spring has arrived, and that means things are going to get busy for Len's landscaping business. He already has five substantial residential jobs lined up for next week. Each involves some planting of decorative trees and installing of other shrubbery on the homeowner's property as well as the performance of an additional chore to spruce things up. Review the clues set out below to see whether you can picture what the workload for Len's crew next week will entail.

1. Len's crew will be planting azaleas at the Jones place, but not a dogwood tree, and they won't be mulching and re-edging the Jones's mulch beds.

2. Neither the Smithsons nor the Johnsons are having Len's crew do any mulching and re-edging, or trimming back of holly trees.

3. Between the Smithers property and the place where Len's crew Is putting in hydrangeas, one is where they will be planting two Japanese maple trees and the other is where they will be laying down tulip bulbs.

4. Len's crew will not be planting a magnolia tree, putting in hydrangeas, or resodding bald spots on the lawns at the Smith place.

5. Len's crew is not resetting the bricks in a little garden path at the location where they are planting crepe myrtle trees or the location where they are putting in some boxwood, nor at the Johnson's (who are getting a redbud tree planted).

6. The mulching and re-edging job is not being done on a property at which the crew will be installing rhododendrons nor at the Smithers place. The job involving the hydrangeas also entails either putting in tulip bulbs or mulching and edging beds.

7. The property that will get the magnolia tree planted is not the one where the azaleas are going in; and the Smithers are not having the bricks in a garden path reset.

8. The crepe myrtle is not going in at the place getting its lawns resodded; and the Smiths are not putting in arborvitae at their place.

		Type of Tree					Shrubbery					Other Work				
		crepe myrtle	dogwood	Jap. maple	magnolia	redbud	arborvitae	azaleas	boxwoods	hydrangeas	rhododendrons	edge beds	lay sod	plant bulbs	reset bricks	trim holly
Homeowner	Smiths															
	Joneses															
	Smithers															
	Smithsons															
	Johnsons															
Other Work	edge beds															
	lay sod															
	plant bulbs															
	reset bricks															
	trim holly															
Shrubbery	arborvitae															
	azaleas															
	boxwoods															
	hydrangeas															
	rhododendrons															

2010S TRIVIA CHALLENGE

Name the popular TV comedy series set in a New York City police station that premiered in 2013 and then ran for eight seasons.

What are the names of Michelle and Barack Obama's two daughters?

№15 RENTAL CAR AGENCY

The BestPrice rental car agency at the airport has five customers coming into town on flights that land in the next hour and needs to get vehicles lined up for them. Paul Prepper, one of the BestPrice employees responsible for getting cars ready for customer pickup, has been assigned to handle this task. He needs to locate the type of vehicle each customer has requested; make sure the vehicle is clean, gassed up, and otherwise ready for the customer to drive; and then put it in the pickup-area parking slot assigned to the customer. However, first, he must decide in what order to handle this influx of customers. Check out the clues below to see whether you can figure out what Paul's workload looks like.

1. The arriving BestPrice customers include Ms. Addison, the customer who booked a small sedan, the person who has been assigned pickup parking slot 40, and the customer whose rental vehicle Paul will deal with last.

2. Mr. Arias has not rented a sedan, has not been assigned pickup parking slot 39, and is not number 3 on Paul's list of customers to provide a vehicle for.

3. Between Mr. Anderson and the customer whose rental vehicle is fourth on Paul's service list, one is getting a medium-size sedan, and the other has been assigned parking slot 38.

4. Ms. Addison's vehicle will be prepped after Mr. Arias's but before Ms. Albertson's.

5. Mr. Singh has rented a large-size sedan and has been assigned an odd-numbered parking slot; his vehicle will not be one of the first two Paul preps.

6. Mr. Arias is not getting an SUV today, and his assigned parking slot is not 41.

7. Mr. Anderson has a lower assigned parking slot than Mr. Singh (whose slot is not 41).

8. Ms. Albertson is not renting a small sedan today and hasn't been assigned parking slot 40; Ms. Addison hasn't been assigned parking slot 37, and her vehicle is one of the first two on Paul's to-do list.

		Vehicle Type					Parking Slot					Order				
		large sedan	medium sedan	small sedan	SUV	van	37	38	39	40	41	1	2	3	4	5
Customer	Addison															
	Albertson															
	Anderson															
	Arias															
	Singh															
Order	1											
	2											
	3											
	4											
	5											
Parking Slot	37						
	38						
	39						
	40						
	41						

THINK ABOUT IT

A study published in the *New England Journal of Medicine* in November 2022 found that there was an observable connection between working on crossword puzzles and a reduction in cognitive decline for people dealing with mild cognitive impairment.

№16 MORNING HIKE

It was a cool, clear summer morning at the state park, and five cars pulled up to the parking lot at the trailhead just before it opened at 8 AM, each car disgorging a single hiker intent on walking one of the park's highly rated hiking trails. The five hikers quickly took off on separate hiking routes once the park opened, but it turned out that each trail they took was roughly the same distance out and back to the parking area as the others. So, they all finished their hikes within an hour of each other, the time differences due to everyone having their own pace, the varying terrains and trail lengths involved, and the time they spent at their hiking destinations. See whether you can sort out, based on the clues below, which trail each hiker took, the time at which they completed their hikes, and the length of the trail they took. Mileage cited in the clues includes both the distance to a destination and the return distance to the parking lot.

1. The hikers included Hal, the person who hiked to Echo Canyon and back, the one who took the trail that measured 6.0 miles round trip, the hiker who completed their excursion at 11:05 AM, and Holly.

2. Harry was not the one who walked the Echo Canyon trail. He finished his hike before 11:00 AM.

3. The Vista Ridge trail, which Hank took, is longer than the trail through the roadless wilderness area but shorter than the trail to Boggy Marsh and back.

4. Hannah did not complete her walk at 11:05 AM, and Holly didn't finish hers at 11:15 AM.

5. The person who took the trail measuring 6.0 miles didn't finish and return to their car at 10:45 AM, and Hank didn't take the trail that measured 6.2 miles.

6. Neither Harry nor Holly chose to traverse the trail to Boggy Marsh and back, which is not 5.8 or 6.5 miles long.

7. Holly didn't finish up her hike at 11:10 AM, and Hal didn't finish his at 11:15 AM.

8. The person who completed their hike at 10:45 is not the one who took the trail measuring 6.5 miles in length or the lakeside trail.

		Trail					Trail Length					Finish Time				
		Lake Tranquil	Vista Ridge	Boggy Marsh	Echo Canyon	Wilderness	5.3 miles	5.8 miles	6.0 miles	6.2 miles	6.5 miles	10:20 AM	10:45 AM	11:05 AM	11:10 AM	11:15 AM
Hiker	Hal															
	Hannah															
	Hank															
	Harry															
	Holly															
Finish Time	10:20 AM															
	10:45 AM															
	11:05 AM															
	11:10 AM															
	11:15 AM															
Trail Length	5.3 miles															
	5.8 miles															
	6.0 miles															
	6.2 miles															
	6.5 miles															

DID YOU KNOW?

Calcudoku is similar to Ken-Ken but was named alternatively in 2008 because of copyright issues. A popular Sudoku variant, Calcudoku/Ken-Ken originally was invented in 2004 by Japanese math teacher Tetsuya Miyamoto to help students sharpen their calculation and logical thinking skills.

№17 BEACH HOUSE SUMMER RENTALS

Dave Danton Realty manages the summer rentals for the owners of five beach houses in Surfside, U.S.A. The houses are all pretty similar, but each has a special feature that helps "sell" the rentals. One day in mid-December, five families contacted Dave looking for two-week rentals for the following summer in Surfside. As each of the houses Dave had on offer was well-priced, and thanks to Dave's persuasive sales presentation, he was able to place each family in one of the five houses that day. The clues below contain some info on the rentals. See whether you can deduce from that info the full story on which family got which house for which summer weeks and what each house's special feature is.

1. Renters include the Andrews family, the family that is renting "Beachcombers" (many surfside beach houses have fanciful monikers like this), the family renting the place with a view of the ocean from its balcony, and the family that will be at the beach from August 8 to 21. The Bascombs won't be staying at the house with the newly renovated kitchen, and their rental doesn't run from July 18 to 31.

2. The Davises will be at the beach earlier than the Carpenters but later than the Bascombs. The Eastmans have an August 1 to 14 rental.

3. Dave leased the Anderson place to one of the families for the July 25 to August 7 time slot.

4. The Davises won't be staying at "Beachcombers" or "Sunrise Vista," and none of the other families are renting those places for the two-week period starting August 8.

5. The Eastmans are not renting the place that has a nice outdoor grill and fire pit. The Carpenters aren't leasing the place that has a swimming pool or the one that has a huge deck. Neither the Davises nor the Eastmans snagged the place with the pool either.

6. Neither the Andrews family nor the Bascomb family is renting the Hardy place, and the Eastmans aren't renting the place with the huge deck.

7. The rental starting August 8 is not for the place with the outdoor grill and fire pit. The Andrews rental is not for the place with a pool.

8. The Davises haven't taken the rental house with the huge deck, and the Andrews family won't be staying at "Enchanted Spell" or "Sunrise Vista." The Carpenters haven't rented the Hardy place.

		Beach House					Special Feature					Times Booked				
		Hardy Place	Beachcombers	Enchanted Spell	Anderson Place	Sunrise Vista	big deck	new kitchen	grill/fire pit	ocean view	pool	July 11 – 24	July 18 – 31	July 25 – August 7	August 1 – 14	August 8 – 21
Vacationers	Andrews															
	Bascombs															
	Carpenters															
	Davises															
	Eastmans															
Times Booked	July 11 – 24															
	July 18 – 31															
	July 25 – August 7															
	August 1 – 14															
	August 8 – 21															
Special Feature	blg deck															
	new kitchen															
	grill/fire pit															
	ocean view															
	pool															

2020S TRIVIA CHALLENGE

This person became the oldest man (at the age of 50) to win one of the four golf "majors" when he won the PGA Championship in 2021. Can you name him?

Name this popular sitcom set in England that is notable, among other things, for being an Emmy Award winner in 2021 and 2022 and broadcast by a streaming service, not a network or cable channel.

Nº18 WHO'S THE BEST QUARTERBACK?

It is the end of the pro football season, and sportswriters are spilling a lot of ink analyzing which quarterback in the league had the best season. Three important numbers to consider in making this evaluation: passer rating (which measures a number of factors determining a QB's overall effectiveness), touchdown passes, and total passing yards. While there is no official "Best Quarterback" title awarded, the consensus is that five quarterbacks included in this puzzle outshone all the others this year. So, based on the clues provided below, see whether you can figure out what the seasonal stats are for each of these five front-runners and determine who performed best in each of the three metrics.

1. Neither Aaron Accurate nor Joe Juker had a passer rating of 102.8 this season; and neither Josh Jetster nor Patrick Passpro threw 32 touchdown passes this season.

2. Tom Teedy threw for a total of 4,919 yards during this year's season.

3. Between Joe Juker and the QB who connected for 4,570 yards this year, one had a passer rating of 104.5 and the other scored 37 touchdown passes.

4. Patrick Passpro, who did not throw 34 touchdown passes this year, did have more TD throws than Joe Juker but less than Aaron Accurate.

5. Neither Josh Jetster nor Aaron Accurate gained 5,134 total passing yards this year, and Aaron didn't gain 5,503 total yards passing either.

6. The QB with a 102.8 passer rating did not get either 4,570 or 4,919 total passing yards in the just-concluded season; and the player with 34 touchdown passes to his credit didn't claim either 4,692 or 5,134 total passing yards.

7. Aaron Accurate didn't garner a 103.1 passer rating this year, nor did the QB with 37 TD passes to his credit (who didn't have a 103.3 rating either).

8. Neither Joe Juker nor Aaron Accurate had 32 touchdown throws this season.

		Passer Rating					TD Passes					Passing Yards				
		99.2	102.8	103.1	103.3	104.5	30	32	34	37	41	4,570	4,692	4,919	5,134	5,503
Quarterback	Aaron Accurate															
	Joe Juker															
	Josh Jetster															
	Pat Passpro															
	Tom Teedy															
Passing Yards	4,570											
	4,692											
	4,919											
	5,134											
	5,503											
TD Passes	30						
	32						
	34						
	37						
	41						

DID YOU KNOW?

Puzzle trivia: The academic study of puzzles is called "enigmatology," and the 29th of January is celebrated every year as National Puzzle Day.

SOLUTIONS

CRYPTOGRAM HINTS

(coded letter + real letter)

1	J = E	15	J = U	29	V = E
2	P = U	16	D = T	30	F = A
3	C = A	17	M = A	31	N = T
4	A = T	18	C = N	32	S = F
5	W = I	19	G = T	33	I = N
6	P = T	20	K = T	34	B = U
7	N = H	21	K = A	35	J = T
8	Q = L	22	N = T	36	J = O
9	B= H	23	B = S	37	D = M
10	P = E	24	C = T	38	N = I
11	Q = T	25	N = A	39	Y = O
12	J = R	26	P = H	40	B = R
13	T = I	27	F = U		
14	R = N	28	B = O		

CHAPTER 1 SOLUTIONS

CROSSWORD 1

WORD SEARCH 1

CRYPTOGRAM 1

A SCATHING CRITIQUE

"Your manuscript is both good and original; but the part that is good is not original, and the part that is original is not good."

—Samuel Johnson

SUDOKU 1

6	4	1	5	7	8	2	3	9
8	7	9	3	4	2	5	6	1
5	2	3	6	1	9	4	8	7
1	5	2	8	9	6	7	4	3
7	8	4	2	3	1	6	9	5
3	9	6	4	5	7	1	2	8
4	3	7	9	6	5	8	1	2
2	6	5	1	8	3	9	7	4
9	1	8	7	2	4	3	5	6

CALCUDOKU 1

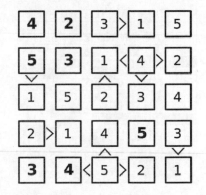

FUTOSHIKI 1

4	2	3 > 1	5
5	3	1 < 4 > 2
1	5	2	3	4
2 > 1	4	5	3
3	4 < 5 > 2	1

LOGIC PUZZLE 1 APPLE-PICKING CONTEST

Adam, South 40, 1,010 lb.

Adrian, Farm Road, 1,130 lb. (winner)

Allan, River Bend, 850 lb.

Art, Old Barn, 930 lb.

CHAPTER 2 SOLUTIONS

CROSSWORD 2

CROSSWORD 3

CROSSWORD 4

1950s Trivia Challenge answers: The New York Yankees (with six World Series wins) – *I Love Lucy*

CROSSWORD 5

CROSSWORD 6

CROSSWORD 7

1960s Trivia Challenge answers: *Cleopatra* – *Rowan & Martin's Laugh-In*

WORD SEARCH 2

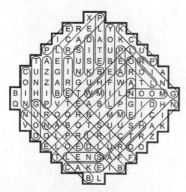

WORD SEARCH 3

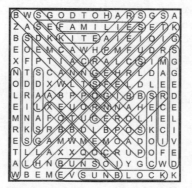

WORD SEARCH 4

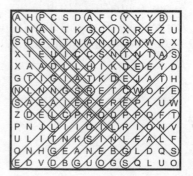

WORD SEARCH 5

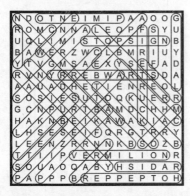

WORD SEARCH 6

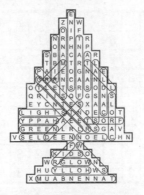

WORD SEARCH 7

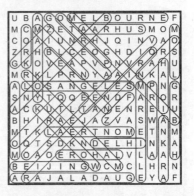

CRYPTOGRAM 2

GET THE JOB DONE
Concentrate all your thoughts upon the work at hand. The sun's rays do not burn until brought to focus.

—Alexander Graham Bell

CRYPTOGRAM 3

GAUGING A PERSON'S ACHIEVEMENTS
Success is to be measured not so much by the position that one has reached in life as by the obstacles which he has overcome while trying to succeed.

—Booker T. Washington

CRYPTOGRAM 4

USE IT OR LOSE IT
Iron rusts from disuse, water loses its purity from stagnation; even so does inaction sap the vigor of the mind.

—Leonardo Da Vinci

CRYPTOGRAM 5

REALLY HITTING IT OFF
Perhaps the most delightful friendships are those in which there is much agreement, much disputation, and yet more personal liking.

—George Eliot

CRYPTOGRAM 6

DEALING WITH OUR LIMITATIONS
To make no mistakes is not in the power of humans; but from their errors and mistakes the wise and good learn wisdom for the future.

—Plutarch

CRYPTOGRAM 7

EVERYONE'S BIG POTENTIAL
Every great dream begins with a dreamer. Always remember, you have within you the strength, the patience, and the passion to reach for the stars to change the world.

—Harriet Tubman

CHAPTER 2 SOLUTIONS, CONT.

SUDOKU 2

4	7	1	2	8	5	6	3	9
2	3	9	6	4	7	5	1	8
6	5	8	1	3	9	2	4	7
5	6	7	8	9	1	3	2	4
8	2	3	5	7	4	1	9	6
1	9	4	3	6	2	7	8	5
3	4	5	9	2	6	8	7	1
9	8	6	7	1	3	4	5	2
7	1	2	4	5	8	9	6	3

SUDOKU 3

3	5	9	2	8	6	1	7	4
7	1	6	3	4	5	8	2	9
4	2	8	7	1	9	3	5	6
5	8	1	9	7	3	4	6	2
6	9	3	5	2	4	7	1	8
2	7	4	1	6	8	5	9	3
1	3	5	8	9	2	6	4	7
9	4	7	6	3	1	2	8	5
8	6	2	4	5	7	9	3	1

SUDOKU 4

7	9	4	5	8	6	2	3	1
2	1	6	3	4	9	5	7	8
5	8	3	2	7	1	6	4	9
8	4	1	9	2	5	3	6	7
6	2	7	1	3	8	9	5	4
3	5	9	7	6	4	8	1	2
1	3	8	4	5	2	7	9	6
9	7	2	6	1	3	4	8	5
4	6	5	8	9	7	1	2	3

SUDOKU 5

1	8	4	5	6	2	3	9	7
9	3	5	4	7	8	6	1	2
7	2	6	9	3	1	4	5	8
2	1	8	6	5	3	9	7	4
5	6	7	8	4	9	2	3	1
3	4	9	1	2	7	8	6	5
8	9	3	7	1	4	5	2	6
6	7	2	3	8	5	1	4	9
4	5	1	2	9	6	7	8	3

SUDOKU 6

9	8	7	5	4	2	3	1	6
5	6	4	3	8	1	7	9	2
3	2	1	9	7	6	8	4	5
1	7	5	8	2	9	4	6	3
2	4	6	1	3	5	9	8	7
8	3	9	4	6	7	5	2	1
6	5	3	2	9	8	1	7	4
4	9	2	7	1	3	6	5	8
7	1	8	6	5	4	2	3	9

SUDOKU 7

2	9	8	7	1	6	5	3	4
7	4	5	8	3	2	6	9	1
6	1	3	9	5	4	2	7	8
9	2	4	1	7	5	3	8	6
3	7	6	2	8	9	1	4	5
5	8	1	6	4	3	7	2	9
1	3	7	5	9	8	4	6	2
4	6	9	3	2	1	8	5	7
8	5	2	4	6	7	9	1	3

CALCUDOKU 2

4: 4	5+ 2	3	2: 1
1	1- 3	4	2
1- 2	4	3x 1	3
3	1- 1	2	4 4

CALCUDOKU 3

10x 2	5	4x 4	6+ 1	3
0- 3	4 4	1	0- 5	2
4	1	15x 3	2	20x 5
2: 1	2	5	3	4
8+ 5	3	2- 2	4	1 1

CALCUDOKU 4

7+ 4	3	3- 5	2	1 1
12+ 5	4	2: 2	1	3 3
3	2x 1	12+ 4	5	10x 2
2x 1	2	3	8+ 4	5
2	5 5	1	3	4 4

CALCUDOKU 5

2	12+	6	8×	3	5
2	1	6	4	3	5
9+ 6	5	9+ 4	2	8+ 1	3
1	2	5	15× 3	4	6× 6
7+ 4	18× 6	3	5	10× 2	1
3	12× 4	1	6× 6	5	6+ 2
5 5	3	2 2	1	6 6	4

CALCUDOKU 6

3+ 2	1	20× 4	30× 5	6	18× 3
3 3	2 2	5	12+ 4	1	6
6 6	3× 3	1	2	5	20× 4
5× 1	72× 6	5+ 2	3	6+ 4	5
5	4	3	13+ 6	2	6+ 1
20× 4	5	6	1	3	2

CALCUDOKU 7

3 3	2 2	12× 6	20× 1	5	4
6+ 5	4 4	1	2	10+ 6	18× 3
1	8+ 3	9+ 2	5 5	4	6
8+ 6	5	4	3	2× 1	2
2	15+ 6	5	7+ 4	3	6+ 1
4 4	1	3	8+ 6	2	5

FUTOSHIKI 2

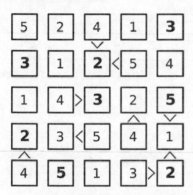

FUTOSHIKI 3

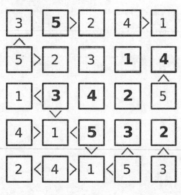

FUTOSHIKI 4

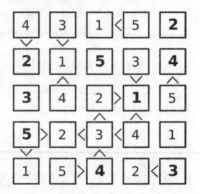

FUTOSHIKI 5

2	4	**6**	**5**	3	1
1	5	**3**	4	6	2
4	2	5	6	1	3
6	**3**	**2**	1	**4**	5
3	1	4	2	5	6
5	6	**1**	3	2	4

FUTOSHIKI 6

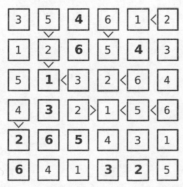

FUTOSHIKI 7

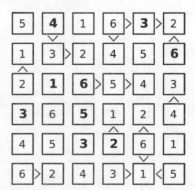

LOGIC PUZZLE 2 CHECKING OUT HOUSES FOR SALE

Top-Notch Houses, 7708 Elm St., craftsman
RE/PRO, 1413 W. 83rd Terr., split-level
Jansten Group, 7417 Elm St., colonial
Smith & Foster, 8196 Upton St., mid-century modern

LOGIC PUZZLE 3 PRESEASON BASKETBALL TOURNAMENT

Bucolic College, Titans, new coach
Hamilton-Witt, Bulldogs, 7'2" center
Midcentral U., Warriors, freshman guard
Upland State, Chieftains, returning starters

LOGIC PUZZLE 4 DOG SHOW WINNERS

Blarney Tom, terrier, white (4th place)
Dashing Reggie, springer, blue (1st place)
Gentle Boomer, Pekingese, yellow (3rd place)
Pamela's J. K., bichon frise, red (2nd place)

LOGIC PUZZLE 5 STRING QUARTET

Sigmund, cello, Beethoven
Stan, first violin, Schubert
Stella, viola, Debussy
Suzanne, second violin, Mozart

LOGIC PUZZLE 6 BEER TASTING

Bridgestone, wheat, 8.5
Denmont Brewing, pilsner, 8.8
Klein's Bierwerks, pale ale, 9.0 (highest rated)
Old Ralston, IPA, 8.2

CROSSWORD 8

```
ATPAR SAME  IBEX
DRAPE IRON  NEAR
HOPPINGMAD  FETA
OPAL  INST SASSY
CELESTA  KIN
  WALKINGTALL
ACRE   AGONIZES
ALIE RABAT  LUST
RANCHERO   SERT
KICKINGBACK
   ORE TAINTED
STONE POOL EURO
TAXI RUNNINGLOW
OPEN ARIA  ARISE
PANG NATL  PIPER
```

CROSSWORD 9

```
CARAT SPAIN  DAH
AIOLI TESLA  ESO
FRUITLESSLY  TSO
EYE  TEPEE SWEAR
  REG TNT ASIA
EDGER PATIENTLY
MARL SAS  MANA
SWEETLY NOTABLY
 GAIA PER  BLUE
WINSOMELY DEEMS
OTOE SSE  PAS
MARDI SAFER EST
ELM PREDICTABLY
NIA SANER EBOOK
SAN ONERS DANTE
```

1970s Trivia Challenge answers: Sam Ervin – Studio 54

CROSSWORD 10

```
OMAR ALAMO  CUED
MOUE PILAU  OSLO
NESS SAINTLOUIS
INTEGER TAI  ATE
 RAMS FUNNELED
SHALT LOADER
HALS PIC ONEDGE
ASI ARDUOUS EER
DHARMA SIT  AMMO
 DEGREE  CROSS
BECALMED  FACT
EVA IAL AUPAIRS
VARIATIONS DOOR
EDEN INANE INCA
LESS CERES ASKS
```

CROSSWORD 11

```
BANS SUIT  BESTS
OHIO ETNA  INPUT
CENTEROFGRAVITY
AMAHL POSES  DUE
 EIEI DELE
GUARDRAIL DORAL
ESTEEM NOD USMA
TAT SADDLED  WIT
AGES SOI SERENE
TENET TACKLEBOX
 DARE USAF
SSE AESOP NUDES
ENDOCRINOLOGIST
TITHE RILE  ELSE
STOOD STAG  SLOP
```

CROSSWORD 12

```
BEET SMA  ASFAR
ACLU CHAR BURMA
GOLFSCORE SPEAK
 FASTING  EDIE
ESTES SOAPBRAND
DARTED  SEMS
IMA ACTI  TETRA
CONSTRUCTIONAID
TASER DUET  ICI
 FRAS  STEREO
CHURCHMAN ONERS
HASA AERATOR
ELITE EASYTOUCH
ALOES TBAR LADE
TENDS SYL  LEST
```

1980s Trivia Challenge answers: Rubik's Cube – Walter Mondale and Geraldine Ferraro

CROSSWORD 13

```
TOBE COLOR  ACRE
AGRA HEAVE  DOER
PLASTERMAN DUDS
SEETHE ALTO  ROT
 SOSA  ABET
DSC REGALLIGHTS
ETHAN OTIS  GOUT
COENS RIN ROUTE
AMEN SALE ENSUE
FAKETHETALL ESP
 ISEE  RAIL
FIN ELBE HEARST
IDEA LACKOFPIES
LOST ETHER IOTA
ELSE RHONE STAR
```

CROSSWORD 14

```
WHERE MOTEL  TEE
AURAL OBESE  REX
SHAVEPOINTS IRE
 EGIS DOS  MIC
PICNIC ASPERSES
ACL AKIN  SNIT
SEI CLOTH SCHWA
SAPS ETHOS HEAL
EXPOS AESOP  FIT
 EMIR MEMO  AVE
WIRELESS ULSTER
AMS IPA  SCAT
LAH COMBTHROUGH
TGI OSOLE INTER
SEP NESTS SEEMS
```

WORD SEARCH 8

WORD SEARCH 9

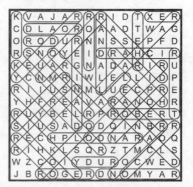

WORD SEARCH 10

WORD SEARCH 11

WORD SEARCH 12

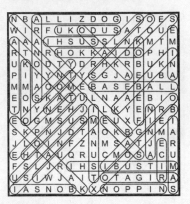

WORD SEARCH 13

CRYPTOGRAM 8

A KEY ELEMENT OF OUR BRAIN'S POWER

Language is the armory of the human mind, and at once contains the trophies of its past and the weapons of its future conquests.

—Samuel Coleridge

CRYPTOGRAM 9

THUMBNAIL SKETCHES OF OUR FURRY FRIENDS

If animals could speak, the dog would be a blundering outspoken fellow, but the cat would have the rare grace of never saying a word too much.

—Mark Twain

CRYPTOGRAM 10

TRUE LEARNING

An education isn't how much you have committed to memory or even how much you know. It's being able to differentiate between what you know and what you don't.

—Anatole France

CRYPTOGRAM 11

AN ELUSIVE GOAL

Happiness is like a butterfly which, when pursued, is always beyond our grasp, but, if you will sit down quietly, may alight upon you.

—Nathaniel Hawthorne

CRYPTOGRAM 12

WHEN ARMIES COLLIDE

The battlefield is a scene of constant chaos. The winner will be the one who controls that chaos, both his own and the enemy's.

—Napoleon Bonaparte

CHAPTER 3 SOLUTIONS, CONT.

CRYPTOGRAM 13

THE VALUE IN KEEPING CITIZENS WELL-INFORMED
Enlighten the people generally, and tyranny and oppressions of body and mind will vanish like spirits at the dawn of day.

—Thomas Jefferson

SUDOKU 8

8	6	9	5	3	2	1	7	4
2	1	7	6	9	4	5	8	3
4	3	5	1	7	8	9	2	6
7	2	8	4	1	5	3	6	9
9	4	6	7	2	3	8	1	5
3	5	1	9	8	6	7	4	2
6	9	4	8	5	7	2	3	1
5	7	3	2	4	1	6	9	8
1	8	2	3	6	9	4	5	7

SUDOKU 9

8	7	4	3	6	2	1	5	9
2	6	1	9	4	5	7	3	8
3	9	5	1	8	7	4	6	2
6	2	7	4	3	9	8	1	5
1	3	9	7	5	8	6	2	4
4	5	8	6	2	1	3	9	7
7	4	6	5	9	3	2	8	1
5	8	3	2	1	4	9	7	6
9	1	2	8	7	6	5	4	3

SUDOKU 10

6	2	1	3	8	7	5	9	4
4	9	7	5	2	1	3	6	8
3	8	5	6	4	9	7	2	1
5	6	4	7	1	3	9	8	2
2	3	8	9	5	4	1	7	6
7	1	9	8	6	2	4	5	3
8	5	3	4	7	6	2	1	9
1	4	6	2	9	5	8	3	7
9	7	2	1	3	8	6	4	5

SUDOKU 11

1	7	6	4	5	3	9	8	2
3	8	9	6	7	2	1	5	4
2	4	5	1	9	8	3	7	6
8	9	2	5	6	4	7	1	3
4	5	7	3	8	1	2	6	9
6	3	1	9	2	7	8	4	5
9	1	8	2	4	6	5	3	7
5	6	3	7	1	9	4	2	8
7	2	4	8	3	5	6	9	1

SUDOKU 12

5	3	2	7	1	8	9	4	6
1	7	9	4	3	6	2	8	5
8	4	6	5	9	2	1	3	7
4	6	7	9	5	1	3	2	8
3	2	1	6	8	7	4	5	9
9	8	5	3	2	4	6	7	1
7	9	3	1	4	5	8	6	2
6	1	8	2	7	3	5	9	4
2	5	4	8	6	9	7	1	3

SUDOKU 13

6	5	7	4	3	8	9	1	2
3	4	2	9	7	1	6	5	8
9	8	1	2	5	6	7	4	3
2	7	3	5	8	9	4	6	1
4	1	5	3	6	2	8	9	7
8	6	9	7	1	4	3	2	5
5	2	8	6	4	7	1	3	9
1	3	4	8	9	5	2	7	6
7	9	6	1	2	3	5	8	4

SUDOKU 14

4	3	7	6	1	2	8	5	9
8	5	1	4	9	7	2	6	3
2	9	6	8	5	3	1	4	7
3	8	4	2	7	1	5	9	6
6	2	9	5	4	8	3	7	1
7	1	5	3	6	9	4	2	8
5	4	8	7	3	6	9	1	2
9	7	2	1	8	4	6	3	5
1	6	3	9	2	5	7	8	4

SUDOKU 15

5	8	1	6	3	7	9	2	4
9	7	2	8	5	4	3	6	1
3	6	4	2	9	1	7	8	5
7	1	3	4	6	2	8	5	9
8	4	5	9	1	3	6	7	2
6	2	9	7	8	5	4	1	3
1	3	6	5	4	8	2	9	7
4	9	7	1	2	6	5	3	8
2	5	8	3	7	9	1	4	6

CHAPTER 3 SOLUTIONS, CONT.

CALCUDOKU 8

12x 3	4	1- 1	2	15x 5
2: 1	2	9+ 4	1- 5	3
10x 5	3	2	4	1 1
2	10+ 5	1- 3	1	2: 4
4	1	5	3 3	2

CALCUDOKU 9

1- 5	4	3+ 2	1	3 3
12x 3	1	0- 5	4	7+ 2
4	6x 3	1	3- 2	5
1- 1	2	7+ 3	5	8+ 4
2	5 5	4	3	1

CALCUDOKU 10

5	8x 2	10+ 3	4	1- 1
3x 1	4	2- 5	3	2
3	6+ 5	2	1	1- 4
6+ 2	1	5+ 4	5 5	3
4	3 3	1	3- 2	5

CALCUDOKU 11

3 3	2- 2	16+ 6	4	3- 5	4- 1
5: 1	4	8+ 3	6	2	5
5	120x 1	2	3	3- 4	2: 6
4	6	5	10x 2	1	3
2 2	3: 3	1	5	10+ 6	4
6 6	20x 5	4	2- 1	3	2 2

CALCUDOKU 12

2- 1	11+ 6	5+ 2	3	1- 4	5
3	5	3- 4	1	2 2	0- 6
15x 5	3	1- 6	4 4	1	2
2: 2	1	5	11+ 6	3	11+ 4
4	1- 2	3	5	6	1
10+ 6	4	1- 1	2	2- 5	3

CALCUDOKU 13

9+ 3	6	5x 2	1	2 2	20x 4
16+ 4	2	6	3 3	6: 1	5
3- 2	4	1- 3	1- 5	6	4+ 1
5	20x 1	2	6	1- 4	3
7+ 1	5	4	2 2	3	12x 6
6	4+ 3	1	1- 4	5	2

FUTOSHIKI 8

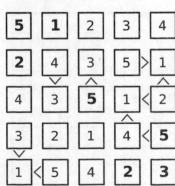

FUTOSHIKI 9

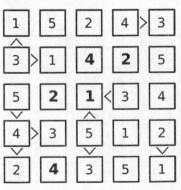

FUTOSHIKI 10

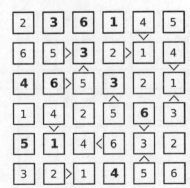

CHAPTER 3 SOLUTIONS, CONT.

FUTOSHIKI 11

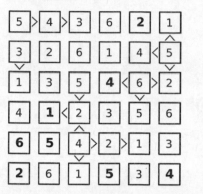

FUTOSHIKI 12

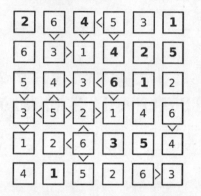

FUTOSHIKI 13

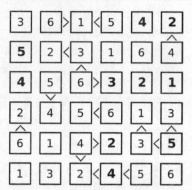

CHAPTER 3 SOLUTIONS, CONT.

LOGIC PUZZLE 7 TRICK OR TREAT

Callie, doctor, 46 pieces, gummies
Colin, cat, 52 pieces, licorice
Katie, clown, 45 pieces, mini-bars
Kyle, ghost, 40 pieces, chocolates

LOGIC PUZZLE 8 A FRIENDLY/COMPETITIVE ROUND OF GOLF

Greg, 78 total score, 37 putts, 1 skin win
Gary, 76 total score, 33 putts, 7 skin wins
Larry, 81 total score, 35 putts, 4 skin wins
Jerry, 73 total score, 34 putts, 6 skin wins

LOGIC PUZZLE 9 GRADING PAPERS FOR COMPOSITION CLASS

Bruce, A+, football team, sentence length
Chuck, B+, housing, organization
Daphne , A, exercise, grammar
Lisa, A–, modern art, vocabulary

LOGIC PUZZLE 10 FINDING A WEDDING VENUE

Country club, June 10, dance floor, $3,200
Downtown hotel, June 24, furnishings discount, $3,000
Historic mansion, June 3, large lawn, $2,500
Vineyard, June 17, free parking, $2,750

LOGIC PUZZLE 11 FLIGHT ATTENDANTS

Pam, flight 2574, 7:25 AM, Chicago O'Hare (ORD)
Patricia, flight 1386, 8:10 AM, Baltimore (BWI)
Paul, flight 3616, 7:50 AM, NYC LaGuardia (LGA)
Pete, flight 569, 7:00 AM, Charlotte (CLT)

LOGIC PUZZLE 12 LAW FIRM ASSOCIATES

Adrienne, third year, Mr. Patterson, real estate
Albert, first year, Ms. Peters, environmental law
Angela, fourth year, Mr. Poston, tax law
Austin, just beginning, Mr. Pierson, business organization

CHAPTER 4 SOLUTIONS

CROSSWORD 15

1990s Trivia Challenge answers: Nelson Mandela – Spice Girls

CROSSWORD 16

CROSSWORD 17

CROSSWORD 18

CROSSWORD 19

2000s Trivia Challenge answers: *Shrek* – Angela Merkel

CROSSWORD 20

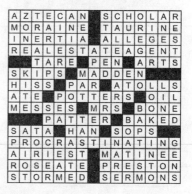

WORD SEARCH 14

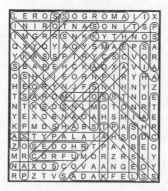

WORD SEARCH 15

WORD SEARCH 16

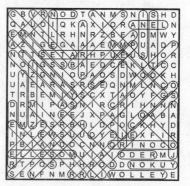

CHAPTER 4 SOLUTIONS, CONT.

WORD SEARCH 17

WORD SEARCH 18

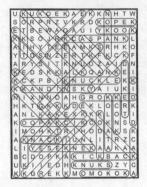

WORD SEARCH 19

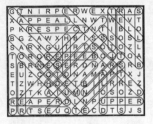

WORD SEARCH 20

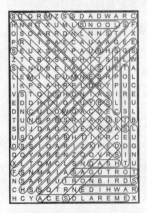

CRYPTOGRAM 14

CHEERLEADING CAN LOSE ITS LUSTER

Although a skillful flatterer is a most delightful companion if you have him all to yourself, his taste becomes very doubtful when he takes to complimenting other people.

—Charles Dickens

CRYPTOGRAM 15

CHECKING OUT UNFAMILIAR TERRITORY

We shall not cease from exploration, and the end of all our exploring will be to arrive where we started and know the place for the first time.

—T. S. Eliot

CRYPTOGRAM 16

USE YOUR FREE TIME THOUGHTFULLY

Guard well your spare moments. They are like uncut diamonds. Discard them and their value will never be known. Improve them and they will become the brightest gems in a useful life.

—Ralph Waldo Emerson

CRYPTOGRAM 17

PERSEVERANCE UNDER PRESSURE PAYS

When you get into a tight place and everything goes against you till it seems as though you could not hang on a minute longer, never give up then, for that is just the place and time that the tide will turn.

—Harriet Beecher Stowe

CRYPTOGRAM 18

PRACTICE MAKES PERFECT

Excellence is an art won by training and habituation. We do not act rightly because we have virtue or excellence, but rather we have those because we have acted rightly. We are what we repeatedly do. Excellence, then, is not an act but a habit.

—Aristotle

CHAPTER 4 SOLUTIONS, CONT.

CRYPTOGRAM 19

MAKING DONALD COME ALIVE

Animation is different . . . Its language is the language of caricature. Our most difficult job was to develop the cartoon's unnatural but seemingly natural anatomy for humans and animals.

—Walt Disney

SUDOKU 16

9	6	4	2	5	8	3	7	1
1	5	3	7	4	9	6	2	8
8	7	2	3	6	1	5	9	4
4	9	8	1	7	3	2	5	6
3	2	6	5	8	4	7	1	9
5	1	7	6	9	2	4	8	3
6	3	9	8	2	7	1	4	5
7	8	1	4	3	5	9	6	2
2	4	5	9	1	6	8	3	7

SUDOKU 17

1	6	3	9	2	8	4	7	5
8	5	2	7	4	3	1	6	9
4	9	7	6	1	5	2	3	8
2	3	5	4	9	6	8	1	7
7	8	1	5	3	2	6	9	4
6	4	9	8	7	1	5	2	3
3	2	4	1	8	7	9	5	6
9	7	6	2	5	4	3	8	1
5	1	8	3	6	9	7	4	2

SUDOKU 18

8	5	9	1	7	4	6	2	3
4	6	1	8	2	3	9	5	7
7	2	3	5	9	6	1	4	8
2	9	7	3	1	5	8	6	4
5	1	6	9	4	8	3	7	2
3	8	4	2	6	7	5	9	1
1	7	2	6	8	9	4	3	5
9	3	8	4	5	2	7	1	6
6	4	5	7	3	1	2	8	9

SUDOKU 19

9	6	2	8	5	7	1	3	4
3	7	4	1	2	6	8	5	9
8	5	1	4	9	3	6	7	2
7	1	6	2	4	5	9	8	3
2	4	8	7	3	9	5	1	6
5	3	9	6	8	1	2	4	7
4	8	7	9	1	2	3	6	5
6	9	3	5	7	8	4	2	1
1	2	5	3	6	4	7	9	8

SUDOKU 20

4	1	2	3	6	8	9	5	7
6	5	9	7	1	4	3	8	2
3	8	7	2	9	5	6	1	4
7	4	3	5	8	9	1	2	6
1	9	5	6	4	2	8	7	3
2	6	8	1	3	7	4	9	5
8	2	4	9	5	6	7	3	1
9	7	1	4	2	3	5	6	8
5	3	6	8	7	1	2	4	9

SUDOKU 21

1	2	3	5	9	4	6	8	7
4	8	6	3	7	1	2	5	9
9	5	7	2	6	8	1	4	3
7	3	8	1	5	6	4	9	2
2	6	1	9	4	7	5	3	8
5	4	9	8	3	2	7	6	1
3	1	4	6	2	9	8	7	5
8	7	5	4	1	3	9	2	6
6	9	2	7	8	5	3	1	4

CALCUDOKU 14

2-3	5	1-1	2-2	4	8+6
1-5	4	3	1	4-6	2
4+1	3	1-5	6	2	0-4
9+2	6	4	1-5	3	1
24x6	1	12x2	4	1-5	3
4	2·2	6	3·3	1	5·5

CALCUDOKU 15

5+3	12x2	6÷6	1	1-5	4
2	6	5÷1	90x5	7+4	3
4-1	9+4	5	6	3	1-2
5	3	2	0-4	6	1
120x4	5	36x3	2	9+1	6
6	1	4	3	2	5·5

CALCUDOKU 16

¹⁻3	³:6	2	²:1	4	³⁰ˣ5
4	⁶ˣ3	1	2	⁴⁻5	6
³⁰ˣ6	2	⁷²ˣ3	⁵5	1	²⁻4
5	⁴⁻1	4	6	⁶ˣ3	2
²:1	5	⁹⁰ˣ6	⁴4	2	²⁻3
2	⁴4	5	3	6	1

CALCUDOKU 17

¹³⁺1	5	¹¹⁺2	3	¹²ˣ4	¹⁰⁺6
5	2	6	⁴ˣ1	3	4
³:2	6	⁶⁺1	4	³⁰ˣ5	3
⁴⁸ˣ4	3	5	³⁰ˣ6	2	²ˣ1
³⁻6	4	⁷⁺3	5	³⁰ˣ1	2
3	¹1	4	²2	6	5

CALCUDOKU 18

¹⁵⁺3	4	⁵ˣ1	5	⁶:6	²⁻2
5	3	⁷²ˣ2	6	1	4
¹⁰ˣ2	5	6	¹⁴⁴ˣ4	3	¹1
⁴ˣ1	¹²ˣ6	¹⁵ˣ5	³⁺2	4	3
4	2	3	1	⁰⁻5	¹⁻6
¹¹⁺6	1	4	3	2	5

CALCUDOKU 19

⁶6	¹⁻2	1	¹⁻4	5	¹⁸ˣ3
¹⁶⁺4	3	⁶⁺5	1	²ˣ2	6
5	4	⁶6	³3	1	¹⁻2
³ˣ3	⁴⁻6	2	³⁻5	²⁻4	1
1	¹²⁺5	3	2	6	¹²⁺4
²:2	1	4	⁶6	3	5

FUTOSHIKI 14

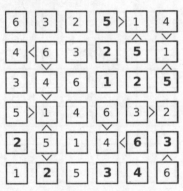

FUTOSHIKI 15

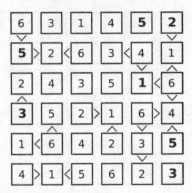

FUTOSHIKI 16

6	3	2	1	4	5
1	5	4	3	6	2
2	4	5	6	1	3
4	2	6	5	3	1
5	1	3	4	2	6
3	6	1	2	5	4

FUTOSHIKI 17

2	6	3	1	5	4
5	2	6	4	3	1
6	4	2	5	1	3
4	3	1	2	6	5
1	5	4	3	2	6
3	1	5	6	4	2

FUTOSHIKI 18

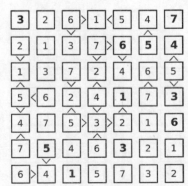

LOGIC PUZZLE 13 PRIX FIXE DINING

Darlene, bruschetta, eggplant, crème brulee
Dave, asparagus soup, lobster tails, key lime pie
Dennis, Caesar salad, ribeye steak, chocolate mousse
Diane, brussels sprouts, coq au vin, ice cream
Dylan, acorn squash, salmon, red velvet cake

LOGIC PUZZLE 14 SPRINGTIME LANDSCAPING

Smiths, dogwood, boxwoods, edge beds
Joneses, crepe myrtle, azaleas, trim holly
Smithers, Japanese maple, arborvitae, lay sod
Smithsons, magnolia, rhododendrons, reset bricks
Johnsons, redbud, hydrangeas, plant bulbs
2010s Trivia Challenge answers: Brooklyn Nine-Nine – Malia and Sasha

LOGIC PUZZLE 15 RENTAL CAR AGENCY

Addison, SUV, parking slot 41, 2nd
Albertson, medium sedan, parking slot 37, 4th
Anderson, small sedan, parking slot 38, 3rd
Arias, van, parking slot 40, 1st
Singh, large sedan, parking slot 39, 5th

LOGIC PUZZLE 16 MORNING HIKE

Hal, Boggy Marsh, 6.2 miles, 11:10 AM
Hannah, Echo Canyon, 6.5 miles, 11:15 AM
Hank, Vista Ridge, 5.8 miles, 11:05 AM
Harry, Lake Tranquil, 6.0 miles, 10:20 AM
Holly, Wilderness, 5.3 miles, 10:45 AM

LOGIC PUZZLE 17 BEACH HOUSE SUMMER RENTALS

Andrews, Anderson Place, big deck, July 25–August 7
Bascombs, Beachcombers, pool, July 11–24
Carpenters, Enchanted Spell, new kitchen, August 8–21
Davises, Hardy Place, grill/fire pit, July 18–31
Eastmans, Sunrise Vista, ocean view, August 1–14
2020s Trivia Challenge answers: Phil Mickelson – Ted Lasso

LOGIC PUZZLE 18 WHO'S THE BEST QUARTERBACK?

Aaron Accurate, 103.3 rating, 41 passing TDs (best), 4,692 total passing yards
Joe Juker, 104.5 rating (best), 30 passing TDs, 5,134 total passing yards
Josh Jetster, 102.8 rating, 34 passing TDs, 5,503 total passing yards (best)
Pat Passpro, 99.2 rating, 37 passing TDs, 4,570 total passing yards
Tom Teedy, 103.1 rating, 32 passing TDs, 4,919 total passing yards

ACKNOWLEDGMENT

I deeply appreciate the important contribution that Patrick Min made to this book—he constructed the delightful Calcudoku and Futoshiki puzzles that are included in it. Patrick is an accomplished puzzle master and oversees the premier Calcudoku website, calcudoku.org. I heartily recommend you pay a visit to the site for more Calcudoku-solving fun.

ABOUT THE AUTHOR

Phil Fraas is a longtime constructor of crossword puzzles and an author of several puzzle books. He also oversees, and constructs puzzles for, a free crossword, Sudoku, and word search website—YourPuzzleSource.com.